Praise for

As Christians we are all called "to
the oppressed free." By stepping aw
oppression of the poor, Bruce Strom gives an inspiring example for ful-
filling this call.

—**Rich Stearns**, president, World Vision US and author of
Unfinished and *The Hole in Our Gospel*

This book combines the clear biblical teaching about justice with practical insights and examples as to how it should be applied. Don't read it
unless you are willing to be convicted and motivated toward practical
action.

—**Dr. Erwin W. Lutzer**, senior pastor, The Moody Church

Wonderful. The stories will make you cry. The biblical material will challenge your mind. The stories of success will thrill your heart. And the
combination of evangelism and social justice is fabulous. An inspiring
book that nurtures hope and action.

—**Ronald J. Sider**, founder, Evangelicals for Social Action,
Professor of Theology, Holistic Ministry & Public Policy at
Palmer Seminary at Eastern University

This book will stir your soul and prompt you to seriously consider what
Jesus' words "Go and do likewise" mean for you personally and practically.
Bruce Strom offers a compelling call to action that no reader will easily
ignore.

—**Carol Thompson**, executive vice president, *Christianity Today*

Bruce Strom aptly points out that most Christians miss the overwhelming biblical call to bring justice to the poor. Bruce's life and message, as
reflected throughout *Gospel Justice*, are the truest examples of godly justice and helping those in need. The world needs more people like Bruce
Strom, and more Christians need to catch this biblical vision of justice
for the poor and needy.

—**David Nammo**, executive director and CEO,
Christian Legal Society

Justice lies at the very heart of the gospel. Through His death and resurrection, Jesus fully satisfied the conditions of God's justice. Now He is
calling us to spread the precious gift of God's justice into every sphere of

life. *Gospel Justice* beautifully proclaims this call to action. Read it . . . and then take up its challenge.

—KEN SANDE, founder of Peacemaker Ministries and Relational Wisdom 360, author *The Peacemaker*

Gospel Justice is a dynamic, new response to God's call and mandate to each of us to provide *justice for all*. Bruce demonstrates how God's commands are addressed to the entire body of Christ, requiring each of us to participate in achieving justice on behalf of the poor. The book will cause you to reexamine your own heart for justice, inspiring you with real examples of lives being changed through the mercy and compassion of ordinary people.

—JOHN D. ROBB, board chair, Gospel Justice Initiative, former National Chairman of the American Bar Association Standing Committee on Legal Aid and Indigent Defendants

Justice is much more than a trend: it is a timeless value that is central to the biblical story and close to the heart of God. Bruce Strom has been a pioneer in challenging the church in the United States to seek justice for the vulnerable in our society, and *Gospel Justice* includes both a much-needed theological framework for thinking about justice as well as practical examples of how that plays out in real people's lives.

—MATTHEW SOERENS, US Church Training Specialist, World Relief, author of *Welcoming the Stranger*

Gospel Justice is a must-read for lawyers and non-lawyers alike. This is a book that will enlighten, encourage and equip you to better understand—and act on—God's heart for justice. I plan to add *Gospel Justice* to my own toolkit to encourage advocates around the globe.

—BRENT MCBURNEY, president and CEO, Advocates International

Bruce Strom has performed a great service to the church through this timely and prophetic word. *Gospel Justice* is both challenging and encouraging. It builds an incontrovertible case for believers to pursue justice for those who are most at risk. Grounded in the nature of God and the call of Jesus Christ, this book is deeply scriptural and very practical. Widely accessible and deeply motivating, Bruce Strom's book echoes the clarion call of Jesus for His followers to be like the Good Samaritan—"Go and do likewise."

—STEVEN C. ROY, associate professor of Pastoral Theology, Trinity Evangelical Divinity School

GOSPEL JUSTICE

Bruce D. Strom

MOODY PUBLISHERS

CHICAGO

© 2013 by
BRUCE D. STROM

Edited by Andy Scheer
Interior design: Ragont Design
Cover design: Brand Navigation
Cover image: iStock 10281937
Author Photo: Administer Justice

Library of Congress Cataloging-in-Publication Data

Strom, Bruce D.
    Gospel justice : joining together to provide help and hope for those
oppressed by legal injustice / Bruce D. Strom.
        pages cm
    Includes bibliographical references.
    ISBN 978-0-8024-0884-6
    1. Christianity and justice. 2. Legal assistance to the poor. 3. Justice—
Religious aspects—Christianity. I. Title.
    BR115.J8S78 2013
    261.8'32586—dc23

                                                            2012050158

Moody Publishers
820 N. LaSalle Boulevard
Chicago, IL 60610

1 3 5 7 9 10 8 6 4 2

Printed in the United States of America

Dedicated to my wife and best friend, Helen,
my sons Daniel and Joseph, my friend John Robb,
my extended family at Administer Justice,
and to my Lord and Savior Jesus Christ,
without whom gospel justice would not be possible.

CONTENTS

Foreword   9

Introduction: Where Is Justice?   13

Chapter 1: Lessons from the Good Samaritan   23

Chapter 2: Lessons from the Injured   39

Chapter 3: Lessons from the Robbers   53

Chapter 4: Lessons from the Priest   69

Chapter 5: Lessons from the Levite   87

Chapter 6: Lessons from the Samaritan   101

Chapter 7: Lessons from the Jericho Road   123

Chapter 8: Lessons from the Inn   141

Chapter 9: Lessons from the Lawyer   163

Chapter 10: Lessons from Jesus   185

Notes   199

Acknowledgments   207

Gospel Justice Initiative

PROMOTE JUSTICE!
GIVE THE OPPRESSED REASON TO CELEBRATE.
ISAIAH 1:17 (NET)

GET READY TO ENGAGE, EQUIP, AND EXCITE GOD'S PEOPLE TO SERVE THE LEGAL AND SPIRITUAL NEEDS OF THE POOR.

GJI.ORG | COMING IN JUNE 2013

/Gospel_Justice   /GospelJusticeInitiative

FOREWORD

I MET BRUCE STROM on a rainy November evening in Chicago. He invited me to serve as the featured speaker at Administer Justice's tenth year celebration. He was working on this book at the time. He shared his hopes with me of seeing the people of God, through the church of God, proclaiming the hope of God, to the poor and marginalized. Bruce shared the dramatic story contained in the introduction. As rain poured outside, the Holy Spirit rained down on hundreds gathered inside that night.

Attorney Strom's heart for the poor is as impressive as his knowledge of the greater landscape in which justice for all is not only lacking in our nation, but tragically lacking in our churches. The second most talked about subject in Scripture, after money, is the poor. And prevalent through more than three hundred verses on the poor is how God cares for the poor particularly because they are the most vulnerable to suffering from injustice. Yet the church has largely been absent in bringing justice to the poor.

Gospel Justice reflects God's heart, demonstrated through Scripture, for the needs of the widow, orphan, alien, and poor. The book provides opportunity for the church, individuals, and attorneys to engage in a powerful, transformative, gospel justice ministry. Through an insightful analysis of the Good Samaritan, Bruce demonstrates that our neighbor is the person whose need you see and whose need you are able to meet.

Gospel Justice is not merely an encyclopedia of the legal needs facing the poor in America and what Scripture says about meeting those needs. The book is a call to action—a call to further Christ's kingdom through acts of justice and mercy. A call to demonstrate to a watching world the difference Christ makes when we integrate the spiritual and the social—the gospel and justice.

Many years ago in Europe sanitariums used to determine whether an inmate was ready for release by placing them in a janitor's closet. Stoppers were placed in the washbasin and the water turned on to overflowing when the inmate was put into the closet and asked to mop up the mess. Staff would leave and return ten minutes later. If the water was still running then the inmate had no capacity to get to the root of the problem.

Much ministry today is spent mopping up messes rather than unplugging stoppers. Justice gets to the root of problems. Justice unplugs stoppers. We don't need messy water flowing through our churches and communities. We need justice to roll on like a mighty river and righteousness like a never failing stream (Amos 5:24).

Bruce challenges the church to unplug the stoppers of injustice. We need to be released to bring justice to individuals and communities in need. There are churches in every community across America. The church is ideally suited to serve as a unified force for change. Will we settle for mopping up messes or will we roll up our sleeves, get to the root of the problem, and do justice together? This book is a great place to start.

The night I met Bruce Strom I also met his friend John Robb. John is a giant not only in stature but faith. Nearing ninety, he continues to press on in the fight for justice for all. Bruce and John were only beginning to put together the structures that would become Gospel Justice Initiative. With the support of this expert organization and Administer Justice, God's church and God's people can engage in life-changing justice ministry for the poor.

As you read this book the legal needs of the poor can be overwhelming. While the needs are great, the opportunity is greater. Jesus demonstrated the danger of missing this opportunity through the priest and the Levite in the story of the Good Samaritan. But Jesus pointed to the power of one person stopping to make a difference. One person can make a difference. Jesus chose twelve ordinary men. They didn't have impressive credentials or connections. But they had a deep and abiding faith that changed the world. So can you.

Don't read this book if you are not willing to ask yourself what Jesus would have you do to further His kingdom. The final chapter is a clear call to action. The gospel is good news to a dying world. Justice is good news to the poor and oppressed. Share that good news. Seek justice. Love mercy. Go and do likewise.

DR. TONY EVANS is the pastor of Oak Cliff Bible Fellowship in Dallas, the president of The Urban Alternative, bestselling author and chaplain of the NBA's Dallas Mavericks

INTRODUCTION
WHERE IS JUSTICE?

I GREW UP IN THE American dream, raised in a small town as the oldest of three sons. My father instilled in us a strong work ethic. I believed anything could be accomplished with hard work and determination. I graduated second in my class from high school and knew I would be successful. By all accounts I was.

Listed as one of the three most distinguished grads of my Christian college, I attended a very good law school, got married, and began building my own successful law practice. I handled cases before federal courts, appellate courts, the Illinois Supreme Court, and the US Supreme Court. I was featured in the *Chicago Tribune*, received several awards, and was making a lot of money. I thought I was a success.

Not really. None of that could fill my desire for deeper significance. I mistakenly believed I was the master of my own destiny. I subtly believed in a God of prosperity—a God who rewarded me if I worked hard, refrained from bad conduct, and gave a tithe from my resources.

God began changing my view through a painful reality over which I had no control. My wife, Helen, and I could not have children.

Doctors, surgeries, shots, and continual tests did nothing to bring us closer to having children. All around us kids had kids, babies were abandoned, and children were abused—but we could not have children. Seven long years we prayed and got no response. I felt like Job: "Though I cry, 'I've been wronged!' I get no response; though I call for help, there is no justice" (Job 19:7).

For years I experienced a roller coaster of anger, bitterness, and desperation. Nothing I did could change my reality. My persistent angry cries wearied the Lord as I asked, "Where is the God of justice?" (Malachi 2:17). Somehow I believed God owed me for being a good, hard-working Christian.

My wife's response was different. Helen did not pray for herself—or dwell on her pain. Like Hannah, she wept in bitterness of soul (1 Samuel 1:10). But Helen also cried that the Lord would take hold of my heart—and the hearts of the children she believed God would provide. The Lord heard her prayers.

Helen and I were at the doctor's office for the thousandth time when we saw two little images on the ultrasound monitor with hearts beating. We were having twins! As we left the doctor's office, we saw a faint double rainbow. Nine months later, on the eve of Joseph and Daniel's birth, we were at a restaurant celebrating when the entire restaurant, including the kitchen staff, emptied outside. Everyone was looking into the sky—at the brightest double rainbow I've ever seen.

I learned that day in June 1999 that God keeps His promises. God answered Helen's prayers. He began a work in me. While I had felt abandoned by God, I had abandoned Him.

I learned God's promises are not for the famous, but for the faithful. I could do nothing to merit His mercy. He had a plan for my life—and that plan was to provide hope and a future (Jeremiah 29:11). I had accepted Christ at age eight, grown up in church, and gained impressive knowledge of the Scriptures. But knowing something in your head is far different than applying it in your heart.

That day my eyes were opened to the promise of hope in the midst of pain. God helped me recognize how self-focused I was, and He helped me see the needs of others in pain around me. God enabled me to begin to understand that poverty of spirit resembles material poverty. The poor also experience a lack of control, feeling abandoned, hopeless, and helpless.

Until then I believed the poor were that way by their bad decisions. If only they worked harder, they could succeed. I thought of them as drunks living under city bridges or welfare mothers abusing the system. They weren't in my neighborhood—and they didn't deserve my help. I had no idea that in a three-year span, nearly 32 percent of people in our country experienced at least two months of poverty.[1] That is almost one in three!

As I sat in church on a Sunday morning, one of the families around me was experiencing some crisis of need. I sang praise songs while blind to the needs of my neighbor. I did not see the reality that most of the poor are poor not by choice, but because of circumstances—like being an innocent child of a single parent.[2]

As I began to see these needs, I knew as an attorney that many of the circumstances causing poverty involve legal issues: from abandonment and divorce to unfair contracts, unfair loans, unfair wages, fraud, abuse, and deceptive practices. I knew that in our country, justice can be obtained only through the law. And the law can be accessed only through a lawyer. Recognizing this, I wanted to do something. On February 14, 2000, I started Administer Justice.

The name came from a Christmas present Helen made for me while she was pregnant: a daily calendar containing Scripture verses about justice. One verse leaped from the calendar and grabbed my attention. "This is what the Lord Almighty says: 'Administer true justice; show mercy and compassion to one another. Do not oppress the widow or the fatherless, the alien or the poor. In your hearts do not think evil of each other'" (Zechariah 7:9–10). That verse would form the heart of Administer Justice.

Our mission is to administer justice through a comprehensive program of educational outreach, legal assistance, financial counseling, and conflict resolution services to empower the powerless, give hope to the hopeless, and show mercy and compassion to those in need.

At first, seven volunteer attorneys rotated serving from the Sunday school room of a church two Saturday mornings a month. I had no intention to leave my lucrative career. I recognized the need was greater than an infrequent clinic could offer, but like Moses my prayer was, "O Lord, please send someone else to do it" (Exodus 4:13). We all want to be part of something significant, but when the opportunity comes, we don't want to step out in faith. Please send someone else.

In such times, God often captures our attention through a person, a radio message, a sermon, or a book. In my case, He sent Jonathan and Denise.

A ministry had referred them for help with a trespassing charge they received while trying to keep warm in a grocery store. I picked them up at a weekly motel and took them to breakfast before court. As we talked, I learned their stories.

Denise had a good family, but as a teenager she did not like their rules and had run away from home. Living on the streets, she did what she had to do to survive.

Jonathan had been a corporate executive. But he lost his job and was too ashamed to tell his wife and left home each day as if going to work. He didn't know what to do—and like many of the poor he chose to do nothing.

Savings were depleted, bills mounted, and one day he returned to an empty house. His wife, children, and furniture were gone. The home went into foreclosure, and Jonathan found himself on the street, where each day became a blur. He had not heard from his family in years.

Jonathan and Denise told me how they felt invisible and without hope. People despised and rejected them. I spoke with them about another man who had been despised and rejected. He was a man of sorrows and suffering (Isaiah 53:3). He had no place to lay His head (Matthew 8:20). His name was Jesus.

I told them that He had a plan for their lives, and this plan offered hope for the future because of His great love, His compassion and mercy. Jonathan and Denise both prayed to accept Christ.

We went to court, and I had the charges dismissed. I plugged them into a local church, where they found a new life and began a process toward restoration in a faith community.

God taught me through my encounter with Jonathan and Denise that there are needs all around us. Those needs include legal services, budgeting help, resolving tax issues, and conflict resolution. Those—along with education—would become the programs at Administer Justice.

OUT OF THE BOAT

I wish I could say that after seeing the significant need and better understanding the poor, I quit my job and went charging into ministry to transform the lives of the oppressed. But I am a boat disciple. Don't rock the boat and definitely don't ask me to get out of it. I would not have given up my security in a high-paying career or my identity as senior partner of a successful law practice if God had not thrown me overboard.

I found myself in the midst of four lawsuits. None was my fault, but my name was first on the letterhead. It was unfair, unjust. And I had been down this path before.

I'm a slow learner, but God helped me see I was like another man in the Bible named Jonah. Like Jonah, I was running from the plan God had for me. The storm of circumstances stopped me, and I asked to be thrown overboard—to leave my law practice to go to Administer Justice full-time. When I left, everything went calm for the others associated with the firm.

While I was not swallowed by a fish, I found myself in the fall of 2002 just as alone in an eight-by-ten office. I would not be paid for five months, as the organization had no money. For many years I lived on a poverty income. Angry at God for taking away my security and my identity, I stood in the office frustrated because I could not figure out how to print an envelope.

"What am I doing here?" I asked. "How did I get here? Is this really where You want me?

Then came the answer. Though not audible, I heard the words clearly and was overwhelmed by the power of God's response: "My will. For whatever you do for one of the least of these, you do unto Me." I broke down and cried.

Some of you have been on long, dark journeys. The challenges never seem to end, and you wonder why. As Willow Creek pastor Bill Hybels writes in *The Power of a Whisper*,[3] sometimes we need to exhaust our energy, our skills, and our abilities so we can hear God's whisper.

I am a slow learner. I am proud. But I heard a still, small voice and responded in brokenness. Since that day, an overwhelming peace has flooded my soul.

Challenges abound as we serve, with Christ's mercy, thousands of broken, hopeless people trapped in injustice. There are never enough hours in the day or enough funding. But God enables us to joyfully hold open our door for all who come.

By God's grace, I no longer work alone, but serve alongside hundreds of volunteers. Attorneys and accountants, financial counselors, retired grandparents, and stay-at-home moms counsel and communicate the love of Christ in the midst of abuse, fraud, and oppression. They answer phones, bake cookies, enter data, mail letters, pray with clients, teach, serve, and glorify God.

Each day is an opportunity to make a lasting difference. I no longer pray for myself or for success. I pray for the least, the last, and the lost. I pray not for my will but for God's will to be done.

But each night I wonder, "Did I do enough?" "Did I make the most of every opportunity in the midst of a broken, fallen world?"

I think about the faces of the more than 4,300 people turned

> I NO LONGER PRAY FOR MYSELF OR FOR SUCCESS. I PRAY FOR THE LEAST, THE LAST, AND THE LOST.

away from legal services every working day in the United States because there isn't enough help available.[4] Even with all our volunteers, it often takes weeks to meet with one of our attorneys. People often drive two hours just to meet with someone for an hour.

In this country if you commit a crime, you can get an attorney. If you commit fraud, abuse, or illegal practices, you are entitled to a free lawyer. But if you are the victim of such oppression, you must fend for yourself. There is no right to an attorney in civil cases.

The purpose of this book is to give voice to the need of our invisible neighbors for justice—and provide practical direction on how you can get involved through education, prayer, advocacy, and possibly establishing a gospel justice center in your church or community.

WITNESSES UNDER OATH

The next chapter will set the stage for the parable of the Good Samaritan, which provides the foundation for what I call gospel justice—a holistic approach that applies God's transcendent truth through just relationships.

If we are to be God's witnesses, then let us take the oath of a witness to tell the truth, the whole truth, and nothing but the truth. That truth is found in the God-man Jesus Christ, who claimed to be the truth (John 14:6). That truth is founded on the whole of Scripture and applies to all people. That truth compels us to just relationships. We must act justly, love mercy, and walk humbly with God (Micah 6:8). We must love God and love our neighbor.

Those who spend time with the poor realize that social justice ministries often do a disservice to our hurting friends. By emphasizing material needs, we sometimes neglect their greater needs, which include hope, dignity, and compassion. And that hope is built on a relationship with Jesus Christ. Like the lawyers in Jesus' day, we give material goods but neglect the weightier matters of the law—justice, mercy, and faithfulness (Matthew 23:23). We must do both, beginning with justice.

A single ministry, or even a network of them, cannot solve the many issues facing the poor. But I hope to encourage churches and ministries to see that justice is a vital part of any holistic ministry—and that justice cannot be separated from law and lawyers.

My purpose in writing is to provide that critical missing piece in any gospel justice ministry.

After more than a decade advocating against injustice, we joined other national leaders to launch Gospel Justice Initiative. This national organization exists to equip churches, attorneys, and individuals for involvement in defending the rights of the needy through legal help and gospel hope. Together we can fight injustice and make an eternal difference in the lives of millions in need. While some may be called to leave their jobs for full-time service, most will be called to volunteer part-time with the gifts and resources God has given them in delivering justice to the poor.

As you study this book, take the time to listen to what God may be whispering to you. I pray you will have the guts to get out of the boat.

Don't allow the pounding waves of this life to stop you from stepping out in faith. Injustice can seem like an overwhelming storm, but God is bigger. "You rule over the surging sea; when its waves mount up, you still them" (Psalm 89:9).

This is a call to action. Parts of this may be uncomfortable. Will you leave the comfort of the boat to step into the storm of injustice? If God can pull this lawyer out of the boat, who knows what He can do with you?

CHAPTER 1

LESSONS FROM
THE GOOD SAMARITAN

"In a sweeping simplification of thousands of years of
Jewish teaching, Jesus summed up God's law in a way that
anyone could understand . . . Love God. Love your neighbor.
That's it. That's the 'Bible for Dummies.'" —Richard Stearns[1]

"And who is my neighbor?" —A lawyer, Luke 10:29

WILMA, A DEAF-MUTE, suffered in silence. The state
took her son, Danny, away. She could not speak for herself, so the
state believed her incompetent. For years she sat alone in an institution, clinging to one hope. She clung to a piece of paper in her
pocket with the name Danny on it. She clung to the hope of being
reunited.

Danny was placed in foster care, adopted, and given the name
Ken. Ken did not blame his mom for abandoning him, but felt
incomplete without her. When he married, she was not there.
When his three children were born, she was absent. He continued
to hope for restoration.

Forty years after the forced separation, Ken's wife found information on the Internet that led to locating his mother. They traveled from Illinois to Alabama and found Wilma—neglected and
alone. When they met, Wilma reached into her pocket and pulled
out the worn paper with Danny's name. As they embraced, Ken
wanted to free his mother and break the chains that kept her from
him, but he had no legal basis. Wilma had no assets. Ken and his
wife were both in ministry and had no means to hire an attorney

to establish guardianship and secure all the legal work to release his mother so they could be restored as a family.

Ken needed more than compassion; he needed compassionate justice. It was wrong that his mother wither away alone, but he lacked the tens of thousands of dollars to file a case, pay for a *guardian ad litem,* and enforce orders across state lines.

Ken reached out to Administer Justice, which assembled a team of attorneys. Judy had experience in elder law, John had a strong desire to help Ken in court, and Phyllis was a *guardian ad litem.* Together they worked at no cost to reunite "Danny" and his mother.

John went on to become a judge. He said this case was the most meaningful of his career. When he took the oath of office, he promised to not only uphold the law, but also to administer justice, citing Zechariah 7:9–10: "This is what the Lord Almighty says: 'Administer true justice; show mercy and compassion to one another. Do not oppress the widow or the fatherless, the alien or the poor.'"

Ken now walks his neighborhood holding hands with his mother. She has learned sign language and can communicate with her family. "I about gave up on the possibility of ever finding my mother or that I would ever be reunited with her," Ken says. "To be able to watch her make me a meal, to be able to hug her, to be able to watch her with my kids, her grandkids, and to see her interact with us—it's the way a family should be on a daily basis. . . . It has literally changed my life and allowed her a life of being a mother."

Wilma and Ken are my neighbors. They live down the street from me, and their walks together remind me of God's justice and mercy. But they are also my neighbors because they had a need to be restored and Administer Justice stopped to help meet that need.

The civil and legal needs of low-income people involve essential human needs, such as protection from abusive relationships; safe and habitable housing; access to health care; disability payments to help lead independent lives; and family law issues including child custody, support and guardianship, and relief from financial exploitation.

More than limited compassion assistance, justice secures the wages of the man wrongly not paid so he can buy his own bread. Justice obtains the child support for the parent to purchase a blanket. Justice intervenes in a housing crisis to prevent homelessness. Justice addresses the systems that contribute to exploitation, fraud, and abuse. And true justice addresses these vital needs in the context of God's justice. God's justice restores. God's justice reconciles. God's justice endures.

ACCESS TO JUSTICE

To obtain justice, a person must have access to the justice system. In America that can't happen without a lawyer. Government and bar association–sponsored *pro bono* efforts provide commendable service. But only the church can go beyond human efforts and provide God's gospel justice for the poor. God can use us to transform the lives of neighbors trapped by injustice.

As we provide His justice for the poor, we can also provide the hope of the gospel. Only the gospel can change lives. Gospel justice looks at the whole person and meets physical and spiritual needs in dealing with legal entanglements. Gospel justice means applying God's transcendent truth through just relationships.

Both the gospel and justice involve vertical and horizontal relationships as we live out the Great Commandment to love God, and love our neighbor through the Great Commission to serve and disciple others.

This book gives a face to our poor neighbor through the stories of real people. It gives voice to individuals like Wilma who have no voice. *Gospel Justice* will examine who our neighbor is, how they come to be injured, why we have missed the opportunity to help them, and how we can reclaim that opportunity.

Why? Why should you read this book?

As an American, I believe it is our civic duty to strive to deliver justice for all. It is not merely a pledge, but a privilege to be part of democracy in action.

As a Christian, I believe the Bible has much to say about God's true justice for the poor—and I believe we cannot fully live out our calling to love our neighbor without a deeper appreciation for God's justice. That is a lesson I began to learn from a lawyer in a familiar story told by Jesus.

RETHINKING A SUNDAY SCHOOL LESSON

Growing up in church, I remember well the Sunday school lesson of the Good Samaritan (Luke 10:25–37). For years I thought of the parable as a simple message of compassion. I did not realize it had anything to do with justice.

I remember the flannel board figures of the kindly Samaritan, his donkey, the man with a bandaged head, and the priest and Levite. But there was someone missing. There was no lawyer. It was the questions of that lawyer—and the fact he was a lawyer—that forever changed my view of the parable.

The lawyer's first question goes straight to the heart of God's ultimate justice: "What must I do to inherit eternal life?" (Luke 10:25). The lawyer's second question, "And who is my neighbor?" was steeped in justice as well, since it seemed unjust to the lawyer that his neighbor should be everyone, including those who seemed to deserve judgment.

Jesus' use of characters from the law—the priest and the Levite—to answer the question would have been significant to the lawyer. I think it equally significant that these characters represent the church.

The injured man suffered great injustice, and the priest and Levite had opportunity to address this—but they missed the opportunity as they walked on by. Perhaps we can all learn something from that lawyer.

I like lawyers. I know that is not a popular sentiment—it wasn't in Jesus' day either—but I appreciate their ability to think through complex issues. I suspect that like others in the crowd surrounding Jesus, this lawyer had followed Him around and heard Him speak. As they do today, I think lawyers in Jesus' day talk with one another. So I think this lawyer had either been present for the conversation another lawyer had with Jesus (recorded in Mark 12:28–34) or heard about it from a lawyer friend.

> One of the teachers of the law came and heard them debating. Noticing that Jesus had given them a good answer, he asked him, "Of all the commandments, which is the most important?"
>
> "The most important one," answered Jesus, "is this: 'Hear, O Israel, the Lord our God, the Lord is one. Love the Lord your God with all your heart and with all your soul and with all your mind and with all your strength.' The second is this: 'Love your neighbor as yourself.' There is no commandment greater than these."
>
> "Well said, teacher," the man replied. "You are right in saying that God is one and there is no other but him. To love him with all your heart, with all your understanding and with all your strength, and to love your neighbor as yourself is more important than all burnt offerings and sacrifices."
>
> When Jesus saw that he had answered wisely, he said to him, "You are not far from the kingdom of God."

That lawyer must have walked away uncertain what Jesus meant by "you are not far from the kingdom of God." There is no reason to believe the lawyer in Mark is the same person as the lawyer in Luke. But they almost certainly knew each other and talked. What did Jesus mean? The lawyers thought they knew the way to the kingdom of God. They must have puzzled over this, and it may have prompted the lawyer in Luke to seek an opportunity to ask Jesus.

"Teacher, what must I do to inherit eternal life?" (Luke 10:25). Put another way, "What must I do to enter the kingdom of God?"

The lawyer didn't just ask a question; he asked "the question."

I can imagine the crowd pressing in. Envision yourself straining to hear the answer to life's greatest question. Like the lawyer in Luke 10, I think I already know the answer.

If someone asked me the question, I would immediately quote Romans 10:9: "That if you confess with your mouth, 'Jesus is Lord,' and believe in your heart that God raised him from the dead, you will be saved."

I would dispute adding anything to faith alone through grace alone and quote Ephesians 2:8–9: "For it is by grace you have been saved, through faith—and this not from yourselves, it is the gift of God—not by works, so that no one can boast."

But that was not Jesus' answer. Instead, like a law professor, Jesus answers the question with a question. "What is written in the Law? How do you read it?" (Luke 10:26).

But the lawyer had heard the professor give the answer before, or spoken with his lawyer friend, and responded, "Love the Lord your God with all your heart and with all your soul and with all your strength and with all your mind" and "Love your neighbor as yourself" (Luke 10:27).

The lawyer wants a discussion, but Jesus simply says, "You have answered correctly. Do this and you will live" (Luke 10:28).

Of course he answered correctly; he's a lawyer. But this lawyer isn't going to let it go at that. Like the lawyer in Mark, he is prepared to justify his answer. He wants to uphold his view that strict adherence to the laws of the religious leaders is the way to enter the kingdom of

> HOW FAR DOES LOVE FOR ONE'S NEIGHBOR EXTEND? THAT'S WHAT THE LAWYER WANTED TO KNOW.

God. As a lawyer, he believes that such a statement as "love your neighbor as yourself" is overly broad.

He undoubtedly thought Jesus could not mean to love everyone. That would be unjust. He means those in the kingdom—the twelve tribes of Israel—not half-breeds who worship outside of Jerusalem like the Samaritans.

I understand.

Certainly Jesus could not mean a homeless person who had made bad decisions or a poor person going through a divorce or an alien violating the laws of the United States. How far does love for one's neighbor extend? That's what the lawyer wanted to know. So he asked a logical question: "And who is my neighbor?" (v. 29)

WHO IS MY NEIGHBOR?

Now we'll get a theological discourse that will justify our position on placing limits on love. Instead Jesus tells a story: A man is on his way to Jerusalem—the center of the universe and true place of worship—when some thieves beat and rob him. Terrible business. That path is a menace. He should have been more careful but . . . Jesus is continuing the story.

A priest comes along and walks past the man. I'm certain he was in a hurry to get home after doing ministry in the temple. He probably wanted to help, but didn't have the time. Jesus continues . . .

A Levite comes and passes to the other side. Very prudent. The man might have been dead—and then the Levite would have defiled himself and been unclean. Maybe that's self-interest, but is that wrong? So far this is an interesting story, but it doesn't seem to answer "the question."

Then Jesus does the unthinkable in the story. Now a Samaritan stops.

What? The Samaritans were a despised minority whose worship customs caused good Jews to shun them—and not even pass through Samaria. And this Samaritan stops and tears his clothes to bandage wounds, pours out expensive oil, lifts the man onto his donkey, then goes out of his way to find an inn where he pays for the necessary care and promises to cover any other expenses.

Who would do that! Who would set aside their own plans (the Samaritan must have been going somewhere), bandage nasty wounds, spend a significant sum, and even promise to return to check on a man who likely hated him? A Samaritan did that? That would have turned the lawyer's world upside-down.

Can you hear the lawyer struggle to respond to Jesus' question of who was the neighbor? "The one who had mercy." He couldn't even use the word *Samaritan*. Then those piercing eyes looked straight into the lawyer's soul as Jesus commanded, "Go and do likewise" (v. 37).

"Go and do likewise." Can you hear those words? That was the answer to the question, "What must I do to inherit eternal life?" Jesus was telling the lawyer he must love God and love his neighbor. Love required action. "What does the Lord require of you? To act justly and to love mercy and to walk humbly with your God" (Micah 6:8). Do likewise.

BELIEF REQUIRES ACTION

Seeing that this command was tied to inheriting eternal life rocked me to my core. Was Jesus really saying I could not merely believe, but that true belief required action? Was He really saying I couldn't just be a good person, go to church, and hold a Bible study on justice and mercy? Did I really have to go and do likewise? Was He daring the lawyer—and me—to get dirty, to serve the broken, to both "go" and "do" likewise?

Yes. The answer was clear. "You see that a person is justified by what he does and not by faith alone" (James 2:24). Jesus was not contradicting His statement that He alone was the way to eternal life (John 14:6)—and that the way was through faith and not works.

But He was saying that true belief is demonstrated in action. "Now that I, your Lord and Teacher, have washed your feet, you also should wash one another's feet. I have set you an example that you should do as I have done for you" (John 13:14–15).

Do as I have done. Serve others. Go and do likewise.

That was His lesson from the moment He began His ministry, unrolling the scroll from Isaiah and proclaiming: "'The Spirit of the Lord is on me, because he has anointed me to preach good news to the poor. He has sent me to proclaim freedom for the prisoners and recovery of sight for the blind, to release the oppressed, to proclaim the year of the Lord's favor.' . . . Today this scripture is fulfilled in your hearing" (Luke 4:18–19, 21).

Preach the good news—the gospel—to the poor. Proclaim freedom for prisoners. Release the oppressed. Do justice. Proclaim gospel justice to the poor and oppressed.

From childhood I understood, like the lawyer in Luke, that perfect justice would be established when the Messiah returned as King to establish His kingdom. Jesus told the disciples plainly what that day would be like in a series of stories in Matthew 25 that ended with His return and the dispensing of perfect justice. On that day, He said, He would gather all people to Him and separate them as sheep from goats. The dividing line was not a sinner's prayer. The dividing line was belief demonstrated in action as one showed justice, mercy, and compassion to the least of these.

> For I was hungry and you gave me something to eat. I was thirsty and you gave me something to drink. I was a stranger and you invited me in. I needed clothes and you clothed me. I was sick and you looked after me. I was in prison and you came to visit me. (Matthew 25:35–36)

Many good people protested, but those same piercing eyes pronounced judgment:

> I tell you the truth, whatever you did not do for the least of these, you did not do for me. (Matthew 25:45)

You did not do what I required. You did not go and do likewise. You did not administer justice for the least of these, and you missed all I had for you. Like the lawyer who received the story of the Good Samaritan, my eyes were opened to the large amount of Scripture that speaks of justice, mercy, and compassion for the poor.

MORE THAN 2,000 VERSES

In his book *Faith Works*, Jim Wallis tells of his seminary days when he and fellow students found several thousand verses on the poor. In the Hebrew Scriptures it is the second most prominent theme—idolatry being the first—and they discovered the two were often related. In the New Testament, one of every sixteen verses has to do with wealth and poverty. In the first three Gospels, it's the subject of one in ten verses; in the gospel of Luke it's in one of seven verses. One of Wallis's seminarians took scissors to an old Bible and cut out every reference to justice and the poor. By the time he was finished the Prophets were decimated, the Psalms destroyed, the Gospels ripped to shreds, and the Epistles turned to tattered rags.[2]

Richard Stearns has written a compelling book that builds on this recognition: *The Hole in Our Gospel*. Stearns was a successful corporate CEO who left that career to lead the international relief and development agency World Vision—motivated by recognizing that comfortable living was not living the whole gospel. Unless we step out in faith to serve the poor, Stearns says, there is a hole in our gospel.[3]

The Poverty and Justice Bible highlights more than 2,000 verses throughout the Bible that address justice and the poor.[4]

How could I have so completely missed the call to action for justice for the poor? Like the lawyer in Jesus' day, I had failed to grasp the signifi-cance of Jesus' teaching on the kingdom. "Your kingdom come, your will be done on earth

> HOW COULD I HAVE SO COMPLETELY MISSED THE CALL TO ACTION FOR JUSTICE FOR THE POOR?

as it is in heaven," He taught His disciples to pray (Matthew 6:10).

That kingdom exists in the here and now—not just in the millennial reign described in Revelation. That kingdom is made manifest in loving one's enemies, in doing justice, in loving mercy, in showing compassion, and in bringing the hope of the gospel to people in need.

I had allowed the world's thinking to corrupt me and missed the basic truth that "Pure and genuine religion in the sight of God the Father means caring for orphans and widows in their distress and refusing to let the world corrupt you" (James 1:27 NLT).

I don't know what happened to the lawyer in Luke. But I do know those same piercing eyes looked into mine. I had to decide. Did I really love God and love my neighbor? "This is how we know what love is: Jesus Christ laid down his life for us. And we ought to lay down our lives for our brothers. If anyone has material possessions and sees his brother in need but has no pity on him, how can the love of God be in him? Dear children, let us not love with words or tongue but with actions and in truth" (1 John 3:16–18)."

Would I give up my comfort, my life, for a divorced woman, a homeless man, an immigrant, or a poor person in need? For these are the widows, the fatherless, the aliens, and the poor. It wasn't an academic question; it was a challenge.

> Defend the cause of the weak and fatherless; maintain the rights of the poor and oppressed. Rescue the weak and needy; deliver them from the hand of the wicked. (Psalm 82:3–4)

And how can we—apart from the law—defend the cause of the weak and fatherless or maintain the rights of the poor and oppressed? Who is better equipped to do that than a lawyer?

"Rescue the weak and needy; deliver them from the hand of the wicked." That sounds like a call to action for a lawyer. To rescue someone like Gabriele.

A MODERN GOOD SAMARITAN

"May I pray for you?" I asked as I always do when meeting a client. "Oh, thank you," she said with a thick German accent. I learned Gabriele's story was a retelling of the Good Samaritan— in which the injured man sues the benefactor.

Gabriele immigrated to this country from Germany. Her husband had abandoned her, and she had done all she could to raise her two children. Without a formal education, Gabriele had made ends meet by doing hair, cleaning homes, and performing odd jobs. Like many service industry workers, Gabriele was often paid in cash and didn't have enough credits to receive Social Security. So she relied on income from her personal care services for friends and neighbors. This was her relationship with Ruta. When Gabriele met her, Ruta was in her eighties and all alone. At first Gabriele would just bring over a meal, and they would spend hours talking. A Polish immigrant, Ruta appreciated Gabriele's cooking and stories from the old country.

As Ruta got older, she needed more help and after a few years hired Gabriele to care for her. Gabriele would mow the lawn, clean the house, cook, and drive Ruta to errands and doctors' appointments. Gabriele faithfully did this until Ruta was in her nineties. When it became apparent Ruta was nearing the end of life, a long-lost great niece appeared. She had her great aunt execute a power of attorney and took over guardianship. Seeing records of ten years of payments to Gabriele, she filed a lawsuit to recover those—claiming Gabriele had exercised undue influence over Ruta.

The suit threatened to take Gabriele's only financial asset—her home. More significantly, it threatened to steal her reputation. She was confused and afraid.

Our prayer together calmed those fears. It was the first of many prayers together as Gabriele went through a difficult trial that sorely tested her faith. But she would say, "Praise the Lord, I have been stretched."

At each step we prayed not only that the truth would be revealed, but we also prayed for Ruta and the great niece. We prayed for the opposing attorney and we prayed for the judge. As we worked with witnesses for Gabriele, we prayed with them.

On the day of the trial we all gathered in the courtroom hallway and prayed. Praying for someone who is wrongly attacking you is not easy, but the effect is significant as clerks, court personnel, and witnesses take notice.

Gabriele won a decisive victory in court. More importantly, with help she was able to keep the focus off herself. She continued to send Ruta holiday cards and baked her a pie, which she delivered for Ruta's birthday. We had spent time talking about forgiveness, and as she met with Ruta, she was able to forgive her.

Ruta died a few weeks later. Gabriele's heart was broken because her friend had never accepted Christ. Gabriele had shared her faith when she spoke of forgiveness, but Ruta would not listen.

What would have happened to Gabriele without an advocate? With limited education, a thick accent, no funds, and an aggressive attorney on the other side, Gabriele would have lost her home and might have been left broken and bitter. There would have been no opportunity for forgiveness, no testimony to the watching world, no peace.

Instead Gabriele knew she had done what she could. Grateful, she volunteered to clean our offices for years afterward. Our offices reflected a life that had been cleaned from the inside out.

JUSTICE FOR ALL

As citizens of the United States, we proudly pledge allegiance to the flag, concluding, "with liberty and justice for all." Yet more than one of every six Americans, like Gabriele, Wilma, and Ken, are poor and unable to achieve this pledge unless someone intervenes.[5]

The preamble to the United States Constitution promises to "establish justice." But as former Supreme Court Justice Lewis Powell Jr. said, "Equal justice under law is not merely a caption on the façade of the Supreme Court building. It is perhaps the most inspiring ideal of our society. . . . It is fundamental that justice should be the same, in substance and availability, without regard to economic status."[6]

So why, every working day in this country, are more than 4,300 people unable to access justice?[7]

As citizens of heaven, we pledge to love God and love our neighbor, then ignore the full needs of that neighbor. Fewer than one in five legal problems faced by our neighbors are addressed with the assistance of a private or legal aid lawyer. And many more of our neighbors don't realize there may be a legal solution to the problems they face.[8]

Why have we, as individuals and the church, missed an opportunity to serve our neighbors in need?

We must not blindly walk on by. The lesson of the Good Samaritan is that in turning a blind eye, we are without excuse. This parable is not only about mercy and compassion, but also about justice. The injured man had suffered injustice—and the contemporary representatives of the church and the legal system missed the opportunity to address that.

> WHY HAVE WE, AS INDIVIDUALS AND THE CHURCH, MISSED AN OPPORTUNITY TO SERVE OUR NEIGHBORS IN NEED?

Today we face a great opportunity to show mercy and compassion to our neighbors and administer true justice. We can address the legal needs of our neighbor with the good news and hope of the gospel. This is gospel justice.

Will we dare to get dirty and intervene in the needs of our neighbor? Or will we choose to walk on by?

CHAPTER 2

LESSONS FROM
THE INJURED

"As a man was going down from Jerusalem to Jericho, some

robbers attacked him. They tore off his clothes, beat him,

and left him lying there, almost dead." —Luke 10:30 NCV

"He was despised and rejected—a man of sorrows,

acquainted with deepest grief. We turned our backs

on him and looked the other way. He was despised,

and we did not care." —Isaiah 53:3 NLT

JESUS HAD PURPOSE in His stories. But we, like the
disciples, sometimes miss the lesson. The first character we encounter in the story of the Good Samaritan is "a man." He is not
given a name or a label because Jesus wanted His listeners to put
themselves in the man's place. If the victim had been a Samaritan
and the hero a Jew, they would have applauded their own sensitiv-
ity for the underclass.

One winter I attended a men's retreat in Wisconsin. I had to
leave late at night to meet with a group helping me submit a brief
in a case before the Supreme Court. More than a foot of snow
had fallen. I hit a patch of ice and slid into a ditch. My cell phone
was dead—and I was in the middle of nowhere. Then I saw a car
coming.

I climbed out of my half-buried car and stood by the road. The
car—with a man in a tuxedo and a woman in a gown—drove right

past me. They'd obviously been at some gala event—maybe even a fundraiser to help the needy.

I climbed back into my car and prayed.

Soon another vehicle—filled with several kids—sped past, leaving me standing beside the road. So I sang.

While I sang, an old pick-up truck came up the road. It was driven by a Hispanic man. He stopped, pulled out a chain, attached it to my car, and pulled me out of the ditch. He did not speak English, but he spoke a language that meant far more to me on that cold, dark night. He loved his neighbor.

That night I was the injured man. You could be the injured man. Yes, my situation was temporary—and profoundly different from being robbed and beaten nearly to death. Jesus wanted to demonstrate the violence of injustice and its effects. He also wanted to demonstrate that injustice is no respecter of persons.

None of us is immune from tragic circumstances: loss of employment, loss of a marriage, an illness, an accident, a natural disaster, a robbery.

Do you know what I was singing as I waited for my Samaritan on that cold night? I was singing my favorite song: "It Is Well With My Soul." It's a true statement of my life, and I appreciate the man who wrote the song. Horatio Spafford was an injured man.

IT IS WELL WITH MY SOUL

Spafford was not always injured. I can identify with him because he was a successful Chicago lawyer. He was even a major benefactor of a rising preacher named Dwight L. Moody. But such generosity and Christian service did not make him immune from injustice.

Spafford's only son died in 1871. Later that year he was financially ruined when the great Chicago fire destroyed his law practice. While trying to sort through the devastating losses, he sent his family to England to support Dwight L. Moody in his evangelism.[1] But the ship collided with another vessel and sank, and all four of Spafford's daughters drowned. His wife alone survived. She wrote:

> We were ten days out in a sailing vessel, and when we landed in Cardiff, Wales, I cabled my husband, "Saved alone. What shall I do?" My husband at that time, just after receiving the terrible news of the loss of his children, wrote the hymn "It Is Well With My Soul."[2]

> *When peace, like a river, attendeth my way,*
> *When sorrows like sea billows roll;*
> *Whatever my lot, Thou hast taught me to say,*
> *It is well, it is well, with my soul.*

What would you do in the face of such injustice? Spafford lost his son, his job, his financial security, and then his four daughters. His wife lost her children and nearly her life. Could we respond like Job: "As surely as God lives, who has denied me justice, the Almighty, who has made me taste bitterness of soul, as long as I have life within me, the breath of God in my nostrils, my lips will not speak wickedness, and my tongue will utter no deceit" (Job 27:2–4).

Could we trust that God was working—even in the midst of injustice?

No external social justice can secure the hope, the certainty, the faith that gave strength to Job and the Spaffords. Only a gospel justice can transform from the inside out, bringing hope and certainty.

Administer Justice opens its doors for all the injured who come, regardless of race, religion, ethnicity, or any other status except need. As they come, we preach the good news to the poor. But not all who come are transformed, for true transformation comes only from God.

We don't know if the injured man ever thanked the Samaritan or if his view of Samaritan people was changed. That wasn't Jesus' point. His point is to stop and demonstrate mercy.

We can learn two important lessons from the injured man. First is the universality of injustice. Second, we must see this injustice.

UNIVERSALITY OF INJUSTICE

Jesus promised, "In this world you will have trouble" (John 16:33). So how does the universality of injustice inform my understanding of justice? First, it should open our *eyes* to the presence of injustice. As we will discuss in the next chapter, this is one of our greatest challenges. We fail to see the needs of our neighbors.

Second, it should open our *hearts*. Realizing we are only a tragic circumstance away from poverty should humble us. We must act justly, love mercy, and walk humbly (Micah 6:8). That means we give up our attitude that we are better than the poor, that we have all the answers.

The poor are not second-class citizens. Tossing coins or used clothes, toys, or other items at them is not what they need. They need you to notice them as people created in the image of God— and to listen to them. Each person and situation is unique, and each solution must be unique to the needs of that individual.

SEEING INJUSTICE

Jesus emphasized that the priest, the Levite, and the Samaritan all saw the man. But the first two just looked and went on their way.

Imagine you are the half-dead man. You see deliverance, but it ignores you—twice. You can feel your life ebbing away, but no one cares. They walk on by.

Poverty is complex. No single factor contributes to its existence, which makes eradication all the more difficult. But the poor do experience universal feelings of inferiority, hopelessness, and invisibility.

The Bible recognizes this invisibility of the poor as well. As Proverbs 14:20 observes, "The poor are shunned even by their neighbors."

Still Jesus chose to live as one of the poor: "He was despised and rejected—a man of sorrows, acquainted with deepest grief. We turned our backs on him and looked the other way. He was despised, and we did not care" (Isaiah 53:3 NLT).

The individuals we help communicate these same feelings. "Getting something free makes me feel uncomfortable," one client said. "I feel like a charity case."

Respect, not rescue, is what we can communicate to those who join us in administering justice. Yes, we rescue people from the hand of the oppressor, but we also rescue to restore to the dignity that is theirs in Jesus Christ.

I want to communicate respect. I want to see the poor. I want to look into their eyes and learn from them. Then I can put together the best plan possible for addressing their issues—a plan that must include hope.

COLD, HARD JUSTICE

Everyone wants to see justice roll on like a river, like a never-failing stream (Amos 5:24). But that is hard when you feel like Job: "But my brothers are as undependable as intermittent streams, as the streams that overflow when darkened by thawing ice and swollen with melting snow" (Job 6:15–16).

Justice, as it's usually practiced by the justice system, does not roll with righteousness, but feels cold and hard. Justice becomes just ice. No one seems to care.

Like Habakkuk, the poor cry, "Why do you make me look at injustice? Why do you tolerate wrong? Destruction and violence are before me; there is strife, and conflict abounds. Therefore the law is paralyzed, and justice never prevails. The wicked hem in the righteous, so that justice is perverted" (Habakkuk 1:3–4).

Jane came storming into my office. "There is no justice," she said. A single mom, she'd gone to court on her own to get an increase in support. The father of her son had an attorney. Jane did not have her paperwork completed correctly. The lawyer belittled her. The judge threw her papers back, telling her they were wrong and he would not listen to her. She left the courtroom crying. Now she was angry at the unfairness.

I listened as she expressed raw hurt and outrage at the man who had left her, the lawyer who had made her feel stupid, and the judge who was mean. "What do you want?" I asked her.

"I want justice."

I said sometimes justice is so cold and hard, it feels like it is just ice. Then I asked, "How are you feeling right now?"

"I'm hurt and angry."

> **"WHAT DO YOU WANT?" I ASKED HER. "I WANT JUSTICE."**

"Cold and hard . . ."

"I guess."

"Then you have lost," I said. "You cannot control what your son's father does, you cannot control the attorney, and you cannot control the judge. But you can control your heart. If you let this circumstance poison you, then you hurt yourself and your son. Your heart will become ice, and you will begin sinking into a pit of despair."

She nodded.

I wrote on a pad the words *sinking* and *justice.* Then I drew a line dividing justice into two words: just \ ice.

"You don't want justice to be just ice," I said. "Otherwise you will be sinking." Then I drew a line dividing *sinking* into two words: sin \ king.

"When sin becomes king in our life," I said, "then we are sinking. But there is someone who is reaching out to save you from sinking. The Bible says, 'Surely the arm of the Lord is not too short to save, nor his ear to dull to hear. But . . . your sins have hidden his face from you'" (Isaiah 59:1–2).

"There is one big problem with sin." I circled the word and pointed to the middle letter. "What is at the heart of sin?"

"I," she said.

"Exactly. I am the problem—not someone or something else. I want things to go my way, and I think I know better than God does. That is sin. Do you see the little dot over the 'i'?"

"Yes."

"That is the dot in my brother's eye, or in this case the judge's eye, the lawyer's eye, or the father's eye. The Bible warns me not to look at the speck in my brother's eye when I have a plank in my own (Matthew 7:1–5). I have a big plank, a big capital *I* that is the heart of my sin, and I need to deal with that first. The only way to change is to realize this isn't about me. This is about what God has for me in the midst of my circumstances."

I drew a big zero. "If I replace this big *I* with my nothing *O*, what do I have?" (s O n)

"Son."

"Exactly. The answer to our sin problem is the Son who loves us and died for us. Now I don't think you want to sink any further into anger or despair. I think you want peace, to replace the icy feeling in your heart with the peace of Christ."

"What's that?" she said.

I asked if I could share something from the Bible and turned to Colossians 3. That chapter begins by speaking about taking the focus off ourselves and looking to God. We all fall short and get angry, but God loves us and died for us so He could replace our anger with His love, through His forgiveness. I prayed with Jane, then helped her with the court forms.

She left that day a new person in Christ, with a Bible in one hand and court papers in the other. She also left with a connection to a church so a community of faith could come alongside her and her son.

Jane had never been to church and would not have sought a pastor, but she came looking for a lawyer to help her get justice. She found a lawyer who helped her understand justice rooted in the good news of Jesus, even in the midst of unfairness.

She wrote later that she lost her court battle but she won something more important—hope. "At the time I could not afford an attorney and was truly helpless. When I met with you, my hope in people was restored. . . . Although I did not win that legal battle, I won something else."

LOOKING FOR JUSTICE

Our nation holds up the image of the Greek goddess Themis as a symbol of justice—a blindfolded woman holding balanced scales with a sword at her side. But for many without the help of an advocate, the scales aren't balanced. Cases drag on in court for seemingly no reason, and justice is anything but a swift sword. Justice often peeks under the blindfold to look at race and economic status. If justice is blind, it is blind to the real needs of people.

True justice is not found in a blindfolded Greek goddess, but in a real God who gives sight to the blind. Justice is not found in a sword, but in the Word of God, which is sharper than any two-edged sword (Hebrews 4:12). And justice is not found in a woman holding scales, but in the Man who removes scales from eyes and who, with arms outstretched on a cross, bore the sins of the world that all who were willing might believe and receive His promises.

As I encourage others to share that truth with the poor and needy, I also seek opportunity to learn from them about injustice. As I stop to address their needs, I must listen to them and I must see them. As I have done this I have learned much about who the injured man is in America.

THE INJURED MAN IN AMERICA

They serve you Big Macs and help you find merchandise at Walmart. They harvest your food, clean your offices, and sew your clothes . . . they are shaped by their invisible hardships. Some are climbing out of welfare, drug addiction, or homelessness. Others have been trapped for life in a perilous zone of low-wage work. Some of their children are malnourished. Some have been sexually abused. Some live in crumbling housing that contributes to their children's asthma, which means days absent from school. Some of their youngsters do not even have the eyeglasses they need to see the chalkboard clearly. —David K. Shipler, *The Working Poor, Invisible in America.*[3]

Shipler gives face to the injured man in America through several first-hand accounts of the poor. We encounter these individuals every day, but rarely take notice. Our nation would be crippled without them, but we give little thought to their needs.

Statistically the injured man in America isn't a man or a minority, but a white single mom with a child under age six.[4] Of the nearly 47 million people in poverty, 19 million are white, 12 million Hispanic, 10 million African-American, and 2 million Asian.[5]

Foreign-born immigrants represent 12 percent of the general population, but 19 percent of those in poverty. And while children make up 25 percent of the total population, they represent more than 35 percent of the people in poverty.[6] The injured man in America may well be your sister, daughter, granddaughter, or niece.

The Department of Health and Human Services for 2010 based the poverty level for a single person as an income below $10,830 a year, and $22,050 for a family of four. One in six people in the United States live below this level.[7] If a more realistic alternative measurement of poverty were used, this number would increase significantly.

Numbers can be confusing. Our poverty line of $10,830 translates to earnings of $38 a day. We live in a nation vastly divided, with the income gap increasing between rich and poor.

Experiencing hardship in a nation where most people face the same hardships can bring people together. But experiencing hardship in the land of opportunity—where the median income is five times the poverty rate—often creates isolation.[8]

Nearly one in three children in this country is poor. Schools across this nation have established liaisons to work with children who have no permanent address as they move from house to house or between shelters. These children feel ostracized. Their parents feel shame because they cannot send their child to birthday parties or the many other events that mark the life of an American child.

We are failing in our promise of justice for all. We are the richest nation on earth with incredible blessings, but when we turn our backs on the poor on our doorsteps, we pull apart the very fabric of our democracy.

George Washington said, "The administration of justice is the firmest pillar of government." That pillar is crumbling when millions of our people cannot gain access to the administration of justice through the courts or the government agencies systems. In 2010 the United States ranked last in the developed world for providing access to justice.[9]

The injured man in America faces obstacles from the outside and from within. Nearly all of these in some way involve law. It is estimated that the poor encounter nearly 62 million legal issues each year and find help for only 20 percent of those.

The injured man in America is a complex composite of society. He is no single race; he is no single constituent. Most work in some capacity, usually part-time.[10] While some struggle with addictions, most do not. Many have low-levels of education, but not all.[11] The injured man lives in cities, suburbs, small towns, and rural areas. You find him in your neighborhood and in your church. On the outside he may not look any different, but inside, like the man in Jesus' parable, he is bleeding.

His injuries may come from many causes. Ron Sider in his book *Just Generosity* identifies these factors:

- ▶ Structural causes, including a decreasing number of low-skill, well-paying jobs; falling wages; and racism.
- ▶ Personal decisions and misguided behavioral patterns, including an increase in the number of single-parent families and other behavioral patterns.
- ▶ Sudden catastrophes and personal disabilities.[12]

All of these factors are true, but they don't paint the full picture. The factors bringing our injured friend to the road of poverty involve external circumstances, internal choices, and frequently a combination. As we will see in Chapter 5 as we consider the lesson of the Levite, it's dangerous to make assumptions about the poor.

FEELING HELPLESS AND HOPELESS

There is a lesson we can learn from the injured man. First, injustice is universal. Circumstances overtake all of us, and no one is immune from poverty. Second, the injured man in America feels helpless and hopeless. He lies beside the road, watching prosperity pass him by. He feels invisible, left out, cast aside.

I felt that way as my wife and I struggled with infertility. Being around people with children made me uncomfortable. While I made a good appearance, internally I was bleeding.

When I joined the ranks of the poor, God so transformed my heart that I did not feel hopeless, but I did feel inferior. As we lived on our savings, I wrestled with not making enough to support my family. It was hard to go from the top of the legal world to what I perceived to be the bottom as a poverty lawyer. The ever-present question "What do you do for a living?" became uncomfortable. I was poor, and I felt poor. Overnight I went from being highly sought to being invisible.

But God had a purpose. I had to learn to walk humbly. I found great comfort and understanding working with those who came for legal services.

God changed my attitude. I realized "poor thinking" could be as self-focused as "rich thinking." Instead of feeling cast aside, my heart was broken for how those who walked past the injured man lost an opportunity.

My identity is no longer rooted in what I do or how much I have. I have learned the secret of being content whatever my circumstances (Philippians 4:11). That secret is what the writer of Hebrews was referring to in the "hall of faith" chapter, which concludes with how these great men and women "administered justice, and gained what was promised" (Hebrews 11:33). They did not gain lives free from poverty, suffering, or challenges. Many were rejected. But when we administer justice, we gain a peace and a joy in the midst of trials that surpasses all understanding. We also gain eternal promises.

We can provide both help and hope. Help through listening, learning, and leaning not on our own understanding as we seek to understand the challenges of the injured—then develop systems that include the law to address those challenges.

We can provide hope through Jesus. Hope based on love, mercy, and compassion. Jesus lived among the poor and spent His time and energy with them. The best place for community is in the church, as we will discuss in Chapter 8. But help and hope can also be provided short-term. Jesus often changed people's lives with a short encounter. Even in those brief interactions, Jesus saw the person.

Matthew describes his sudden encounter with Jesus. "As Jesus went on from there, *he saw* a man named Matthew sitting at the tax collector's booth" (Matthew 9:9, emphasis added). Jesus saw Matthew. While Matthew was not materially poor, he was poor and bleeding. This is why, when the Pharisees challenged Jesus' reaching out to Matthew, Jesus said, "It is not the healthy who need a doctor, but the sick. But go and learn what this means: 'I desire mercy, not sacrifice.' For I have not come to call the righteous, but sinners" (Matthew 9:12–13).

The injured man needs to be seen. Don't pass him by. Don't patronize him. Develop a relationship. Listen and learn from him. Discover his needs, discover his talents, then help develop those skills as you assist in overcoming legal and other barriers.

On some level, you too are the injured man. You and he are both bleeding from the effects of sin in this world. So act justly, show mercy, and walk humbly beside your neighbor in need. This is the lesson of the injured man.

CHAPTER 3

LESSONS FROM
THE ROBBERS

"As a man was going down from Jerusalem to Jericho, some
robbers attacked him. They tore off his clothes, beat him,
and left him lying there, almost dead." —Luke 10:30 NCV

"Who will protect me from the wicked? Who will stand
up for me against evildoers? . . . They crush your people,
Lord, hurting those you claim as your own. They kill
widows and foreigners and murder orphans. 'The Lord isn't
looking,' they say, 'and besides, the God of Israel doesn't
care.'" —Psalm 94:16, 5–7 NLT

WE DON'T SEE THEM in the story, but the effect of
their presence is painfully clear—the robbers of justice. They steal,
beat, and take what they want because they don't believe anyone
will challenge them. For the robbers, the Lord isn't looking and
doesn't care.

The robbers of justice prey on the weak in innumerable ways.
You may not see them, but their passing is unmistakable.

During the housing boom, they set up predatory loans, shaded
the truth on applicant income, inflated appraisals, and played on
the dream to own a home that was really too expensive. When the
housing market collapsed, they set up businesses to "save" people
from foreclosure while buying houses out from under them. Government plans to help were complex and inadequately funded.
Few loans were modified, short sales took too long to approve,
and more people lost their homes. The robbers are opportunistic,

and fraud continues to rise in the mortgage industry as the law struggles to keep up with the challenges.[1] Not surprisingly many of the victims are elderly and minorities.[2]

Robbers of justice establish payday lending establishments in low-income and minority neighborhoods. In Chicago, there is one payday lending establishment for every 463 poor families, compared to one McDonald's restaurant for every 780 poor Chicago families.[3] These lenders provide the poor with ready cash—borrowed against wages before they are received. If there is any problem with repayment, these lenders roll the loan over and charge upward of 700 percent interest.[4]

Other robbers prey on the poor's need for tax refunds by providing refund anticipation loans. They lure consumers in, charging unnecessary fees to prepare simple returns, then charge interest rates ranging from 77 to 140 percent.[5] In 2006, the poor lost $900 million in such loans.[6]

As the government seeks to help the poor through the often-confusing earned income tax credit, the robbers strip the poor of these benefits by enticing them to get money now rather than wait the average of ten days to get a direct deposit refund from the government. Many of these robbers have no background in tax, but they set up shop and promise refunds frequently based on incorrect credits and deductions. When the IRS notice arrives challenging the incorrect returns, the tax preparers are nowhere to be found. Now the poor are additionally penalized with money owed, interest, and penalties.

As the poor seek help to resolve these issues, they see commercials encouraging them to call and settle IRS debt for pennies on the dollar. Several of our tax clients, lured by such promises, have paid thousands of dollars only to receive no help and be further victimized.

Innocent spouses, who signed tax returns not knowing they

contained unreported income or improper deductions, receive notices threatening to attach assets years later. Still hurting from a
divorce, they now must face the IRS. Without help they would be
required to pay money they do not have, toward a debt for which
they were not responsible.

Robbers also engage in identity theft. Terrified by the letters
from the IRS, Mabel, a dear eighty-two-year-old woman, brought
them in to our office unopened with shaking hands. She came
because the IRS was garnishing her Social Security payments. She
didn't understand what was happening, and now she didn't have
enough money to meet her basic needs. She could not sleep for
fear the IRS would throw her in jail. Working with the taxpayer
advocate service, we stopped the garnishment while determining
the issue, which arose from someone having obtained her Social
Security number.

Other robbers sell used vehicles with loans carrying interest
rates of 40 or 50 percent. Juan purchased a truck for $24,000. Af-
ter nearly four years of regular payments, he still owed $22,000.
Without the intervention of an attorney, he would have eventually
paid more than $50,000.

Robbers exploit workers by paying unfair wages or no wages.
They issue credit cards like candy and switch interest rates and add
additional fees and penalties. They establish investment schemes
with the promise of a quick return.

Robbers are everywhere, looking to make money off fear, false
hope, lack of options, and misinformation. Their victims are poor,
disadvantaged, elderly, minorities, and people with low education.
And all too often the oppressors are people of the same race, speak
the same language, or claim the same faith—then take unfair advantage of the trust that engenders.

LESSON ONE: GET EDUCATED

One of the first lessons we learn from the robbers is the need to educate ourselves and the poor, so we are empowered to stand against financial exploitation. Our office goes into the community working with churches, schools, and community organizations to bring information to the people and empower them to avoid these problems.

Oppression is motivated not only by greed, but also by power. Not content with fraud, oppressors often commit violence. The robbers in Luke could have simply taken the man's cloak and his money. But they beat him and left him for dead.

LESSON TWO: INJUSTICE IS VIOLENT

The news is filled with stories of senseless crime as people rob and abuse one another. As horrific as this is, worse is the kind that takes place closer to home and usually goes unreported: elder abuse, child abuse, and domestic partner abuse.

At some point in their lives, an estimated one in four women and one in nine men in the United States are victims of domestic violence.[7] In households with incomes under $15,000 per year, 35.5 percent of women and 20.7 percent of men suffer violence from an intimate partner.[8] Each year, intimate partner violence results in an estimated 1,200 deaths and two million injuries among women and nearly 600,000 injuries among men.[9]

And the violence extends to the most vulnerable in society—children and the elderly. According to the best estimates, between one and two million Americans age 65 or older have been injured, exploited, or otherwise mistreated by someone on whom they depend for care or protection.[10] And for every reported case, another five go unreported.[11]

And children are even more vulnerable as victims of neglect, abuse, sexual assault, maltreatment, abandonment, and medical neglect. The highest incidence occurs to children less than a year old, and nearly one-third of all victims are younger than four.[12] Nearly half of all victims are white. Only 9 percent of perpetrators were strangers to the child, with 81 percent being a parent.[13] Some older children flee this—only to find themselves on the streets and trapped in further abuse.

> Why, O Lord, do you stand far off? Why do you hide yourself in times of trouble? In his arrogance the wicked man hunts down the weak, who are caught in the schemes he devises. (Psalm 10:1–2)

This is the cry of the oppressed. The wicked are arrogant because they believe no one cares for the poor. They believe God does not see or care.

They are wrong. Dozens of verses cry out against injustice: "For I, the Lord, love justice; I hate robbery and iniquity" (Isaiah 61:8).[14] This is what God sees:

> The people of the land practice extortion and commit robbery; they oppress the poor and needy and mistreat the alien, denying them justice. I looked for a man among them who would build up the wall and stand before me in the gap on behalf of the land so I would not have to destroy it, but I found none. (Ezekiel 22:29–30)

Who will stand in the gap on behalf of Rita? An older Filipino who had come to this country to earn a decent wage and have benefits for her husband, who had several health problems, Rita worked hard at her low-wage job without complaining.

Her husband received excellent medical care, but then they started receiving bills they could not pay. They found themselves being sued. Rita had been taught not to question authority. She assumed she owed the money, but did not know how she could pay. She came to see Jim, a volunteer financial counselor.

Jim prayed with Rita and her husband and helped put them at ease. As he examined the bills, he could find no payments by the insurance company. He examined the pay stubs and found insurance being deducted, so he asked if they knew why the insurance company had not paid.

Rita spoke no English. She assumed that when she provided the information to the doctors and hospital, all would be resolved—and that if she received a bill, she owed it. Jim made a call and discovered no insurance premiums had ever been paid. The employer had been keeping the money, assuming an older immigrant who did not speak the language would not do anything.

Jim involved our attorneys, who filed an action requiring the employer to become a party to the lawsuit, which exonerated Rita of any responsibility and placed it on the employer.

LESSON THREE: RESCUE FROM THE HAND OF THE OPPRESSOR

"This is what the Lord says: 'Administer justice every morning; rescue from the hand of his oppressor the one who has been robbed, or my wrath will break out and burn like fire because of the evil you have done—burn with no one to quench it" (Jeremiah 21:12). Jim administered justice. So did Scott.

Scott was a young attorney volunteer when he met Garret, an older white man who was disabled. He hadn't always been disabled; an uninsured driver struck his car, leaving him with permanent brain damage. He now lived in subsidized housing.

His landlord could make more money renting to someone else and served an eviction notice, claiming Garret failed to pay the rent. Garret was certain he had paid, but was confused and his slurred speech made it difficult to answer the allegations. Scott went to Garret's bank to obtain proof of the payment, which was presented in court—only to have the landlord claim he made an error and that a different month had gone unpaid.

Scott returned to the bank for proof of payment, and this time he received a decisive victory in court. Had Garret been evicted, he could not have obtained subsidized housing elsewhere and would have become homeless. Without legal assistance, the cost of two court hearings and obtaining the records would have been thousands of dollars—well outside Garret's reach. Without Christian legal assistance, Garret would not have received hope. "Thank God," he said, "I got some help."

Like Jim and Scott, hundreds of others serve because they know "the Lord secures justice for the poor and upholds the cause of the needy" (Psalm 140:12). God sees, and He sends His servants to secure justice. "But you, O God, do see trouble and grief; you consider it to take it in hand. The victim commits himself to you; you are the helper of the fatherless. Break the arm of the wicked and evil man; call him to account for his wickedness that would not be found out" (Psalm 10:14–15).

Our office does not stand alone. Another fighter against injustice is Gary Haugen.

Gary was an attorney with a comfortable life serving in the US Department of Justice. While there he saw the incredible injustice in the world in human trafficking, and recognized government alone could not do all that was needed. Realizing there was a role for Christian attorneys and the church, he began International Justice Mission (IJM).

Today IJM is a powerful agent in combating injustice around the world. Haugen's most recent book, *Just Courage*, sounds a strong call to action against the robbers of justice internationally. But similar robbers also operate in America.

> THE ROBBERS OF JUSTICE DON'T WANT US TO SEE. *TURN A BLIND EYE,* THEY SAY.

The robbers of justice don't want us to see. *Turn a blind eye,* they say, *so we can continue to oppress.* In America the robbers often succeed because we do not want to believe these crimes take place on our shores.

For the first time, in 2010, the United States was added to the list of nations dealing with the issue of trafficking in persons.[15] The State Department finally recognized the injustices that exist in our own neighborhoods:

> The United States is a source, transit, and destination country for men, women, and children subjected to trafficking in persons, specifically forced labor, debt bondage, and forced prostitution. Trafficking occurs primarily for labor and most commonly in domestic servitude, agriculture, manufacturing, janitorial services, hotel services, construction, health and elder care, hair and nail salons, and strip club dancing. Vulnerabilities remain even for legally documented temporary workers who typically fill labor needs in the hospitality, landscaping, construction, food service, and agricultural industries.[16]

The robbers bring sex slaves, domestic slaves, and laborers to this country under false promises. They exploit the vulnerable on the assumption that no one is looking, no one cares.

Chantou was brought to the U.S. from Cambodia for an arranged marriage. Though married, she had no relationship with her "husband," who instead sold her to different men. After a year of this, a friend rallied her church to provide a home and protection for her. The moment Chantou's "husband" realized this, he fled the country.

But what was a disgraced young woman to do? Without an adjusted immigration status, she would not be able to live and work in the U.S. If deported, she would be a disgraced outcast and not able to return home for fear of death. In America she was still married and would remain, in the eyes of the law, chained to her "husband" forever.

Food and shelter assistance alone would not help Chantou. She needed a lawyer. Finding an advocate made all the difference.

Maria was thirteen when she entered the United States. Her father had died and her mother abandoned her. Alone in Mexico, she had no future. With relatives in the U.S., she accepted a nice man's offer to bring her to America. After he sexually abused her, he sold her to a cantina where drugs, alcohol, and men dulled her senses and threatened to destroy her. But her relatives tracked her down and rescued her.

Undocumented, Maria was afraid, not knowing what to do. She found us, and we helped her face her oppressors for prosecution and obtain a special trafficking visa (T-visa) to establish lawful residence in the United States. Maria now has a new outlook on life: "They gave me hope that there can be justice for everyone—even someone like me."

Jorge was Mexican. He worked hard as a roofer, but his employer refused to pay him. Regardless of how one feels about undocumented workers, the exploitation of laborers is wrong. "Do not take advantage of a hired man who is poor and needy, whether he is a brother Israelite or an alien living in one of your towns" (Deuteronomy 24:14).

Without legal intervention, Jorge and many others would be victims of unfair labor practices. While Jorge and others might find help at a food pantry or shelter, what they really need is justice—a fair wage for work performed—so they can support themselves. That is not possible without the help of an attorney.

LESSON FOUR: BEWARE THE GOLDEN CLUB

There is a robber inside each of us. If not careful, any of us can twist the golden rule into the golden club and do unto others as they have done unto us. Sometimes we need to help someone see why the end they are pursuing is not just. Most of the time we see people who are simply caught in a complex system they do not understand.

Sabrina suffers from a disability. Her employer no longer felt she was capable of doing her job and fired her. All of Sabrina's job performance reviews had been excellent, so she assumed she would receive unemployment compensation. She had a phone hearing, where she was surprised the employer had an attorney. She was further surprised by allegations that she was dismissed for cause. She didn't even know how to respond—and was denied the unemployment she needed to support herself and her son.

She tried to call attorneys, but no one would talk to her unless she could pay significant money up front. Finally she found help at our office.

Agnes, a volunteer attorney who immigrated to this country from Poland, had great compassion and was grateful she could use her skills to stand up for Sabrina. The case went to trial, and Sabrina was vindicated. Her dignity and her benefits were restored.

For the next several months, Sabrina volunteered for us. We included her and her son in office events, and she became a part of our extended family as she grew in her faith and found herself encouraging others.

LESSON FIVE: THE SYSTEM CAN BE A ROBBER

Sometimes even our justice system can become a party to robbery. Carol had a five-year-old son whose father was an abusive alcoholic. But he made good money, and she earned very little as a waitress. Carol gave the father an ultimatum to stop drinking or leave. He went straight to the courthouse, where he met with a legal aid organization and sought a domestic violence order against Carol. While the order was not granted, the father had created a conflict of interest, so the organization could not represent Carol. Then he hired an aggressive attorney and filed for custody of his son. If the community hadn't had another legal organization for the poor, Carol would have lost her son.

"I looked and saw all the oppression that was taking place under the sun: I saw the tears of the oppressed—and they have no comforter; power was on the side of their oppressors—and they have no comforter" (Ecclesiastes 4:1).

Beth stood in the doorway of her home crying as police escorted her children away from her. She didn't know what was happening. The police gave her papers and shoved her two young children into the back of a squad car and drove away.

Beth could not believe the papers. Her estranged husband had filed domestic violence papers alleging she was abusing the children by not spraying them with mosquito repellant, subjecting them to possible West Nile virus. The only other allegation was that she was planning to go to Mexico, even though all her family lived locally and she was Caucasian.

Beth felt certain she simply needed to tell the judge her story. She had no money, so she went to court on her own. Her husband had an attorney, who kept objecting to anything she tried to say, twisting her words. Beth got upset, and the judge ruled against her. It was his last day on the bench, and he had no patience for unrepresented people. Beth suddenly found herself without her children.

Her daughter had special needs, requiring medication the father refused to give. Dad didn't want the children around him and his new girlfriend, so he dropped them off at the laundromat where his mother worked; it was Grandma who really wanted the kids and was paying for the lawyer.

Beth found herself in a custody battle for her own children, with the system stacked against her. Her mom brought her to Administer Justice, where an advocate helped get a neutral guardian appointed. The case was resolved, but only after a trial.

The guardian, who later become a judge, called it the worst case of injustice he had seen in thirty years. Today the children are safe with their mother. Beth had not been part of a church community, but today she is an active part of her church's gospel choir.

We have helped parents falsely accused of hurting their children as the state took them from their care, and parents whose children were taken away for various trivial reasons. Too often the system simply allows children to be ripped from the home, assuming everything will later get sorted out. But where do parents with limited resources go for help?

Where do dads go when they just want to have a relationship with their children, but are falsely accused by moms motivated by hatred for the father instead of love for the child?

And who rescues the child from the hand of an abusive parent? Shane was six. His father had spent most of Shane's life in jail, and his mother turned to alcohol and drugs and often neglected her son. Shane's uncle Sal wanted to help his nephew, but did not know how. He knew the boy was in danger and did not want to wait until the state stepped in. We were able to help him establish guardianship and create a home for Shane—free from uncertainty and abuse.

LESSON SIX: INJUSTICE SCARS

Would the injured man bear the scars of the beating for the rest of his life? Maybe. It takes a long time for such wounds to heal. It did for Maura.

Maura was brought to our office by a concerned church friend. A small woman with black hair and distinct Italian features, Maura was disabled and suffered from epilepsy. When I first met Maura she could not look me in the eye. She wrung her hands and looked at the floor as she explained the horrible abuse she had suffered from her husband. Then she had endured a painful trial, in which the testimony about the abuse was so profound, the court ordered the father to receive counseling before he could see his daughter. The father refused.

Two years later the father returned to court, wanting to know where his ex and daughter lived. Terrified, Maura described how she lived with the shades pulled down, and would not let her nine-year-old daughter go outside for fear the father would kidnap her. She could not get through more than a sentence before a seizure would freeze her in a brief catatonic state. We prayed and she cried.

Over the next nine years we were in and out of court as her ex-husband refused to pay her support. Six times he was held in contempt of court and compelled to pay or go to jail. Along the way we had many discussions of God's plan for Maura's life and for her daughter. Maura struggled with breast cancer and survived. Her epileptic seizures improved dramatically. She found new hope.

Maura went to school to become a pastry chef. At later court hearings she would bake Italian cookies and bring them to court. She learned to stand tall, to smile, and received a renewed faith in God and in man. Her daughter did extremely well in school and attended college. None of that may have happened without the help of caring attorneys who came alongside Maura, serving her with the hope of the gospel.

Today Maura knows it is God who rescued her, and she joins the psalmist in saying, "My whole being will exclaim, 'Who is like you, O Lord? You rescue the poor from those too strong for them, the poor and needy from those who rob them'" (Psalm 35:10).

The justice robbers think they can hide behind rocks waiting for their victims. Injustice is a mountain. But God is bigger. Justice is bigger. "But the Lord has become my fortress; and my God the rock in whom I take refuge" (Psalm 94:22). There is hope in the mighty rock of justice. He is able to save. That is the message of gospel justice and how God is defending the weak, the poor, and the vulnerable against the robbers.

LESSON SEVEN: INJUSTICE IS EVIL

The final lesson of the robbers is that evil is real. There are evil forces at work in the world. "We are not fighting against humans. We are fighting against forces and authorities and against rulers of darkness and powers in the spiritual world" (Ephesians 6:12 CEV).

Robbers attack under the cover of darkness. The robbers don't want us to see. They tell us to pass on by. Don't listen. But we are called to "have nothing to do with the fruitless deeds of darkness, but rather expose them" (Ephesians 5:11).

"Woe to those who go to great depths to hide their plans from the Lord, who do their work in darkness and think, 'Who sees us? Who will know?'" (Isaiah 29:15).

God knows. Into such darkness He spoke. "The people walking in darkness have seen a great light; on those living in the land of the shadow of death a light has dawned" (Isaiah 9:2).

That light was the light of salvation through Jesus. He is the light of the world, and if we are to dispel the darkness we must do so with the light of the gospel. The way to provide true hope is through the rich promises of God: "I will turn the darkness into light before them and make the rough places smooth. These are the things I will do; I will not forsake them" (Isaiah 42:16).

But we do not bring the gospel alone. "Your desire to tell the good news about peace should be like shoes on your feet" (Ephesians 6:15 CEV). We must "be ready! Let the truth be like a belt around your waist, and let God's justice protect you like armor" (Ephesians 6:14 CEV).

It is God's justice that makes a way in the darkness of oppression, but He commands us to put on our armor and get in the fight. He tells us if you "satisfy the needs of the oppressed, then your light will rise in the darkness, and your night will become like the noonday" (Isaiah 58:10).

This is the message of gospel justice that brings both truth and action to battle the robbers of injustice. May we battle the forces of darkness through the power of light, through prayer, and courageous action.

Lord, give us eyes that we may see the needs around us. Give us courage to confront injustice. Give us wisdom to educate ourselves and others. Give us discernment that we not become robbers using a golden club. Give us righteous anger to combat evil. And give us holy hands raised in prayer against the spiritual forces of darkness wherever they may be found.

CHAPTER 4

LESSONS FROM
THE PRIEST

"By chance a priest came along. But when he saw
the man lying there, he crossed to the other side
of the road and passed him by." —Luke 10:31 NLT

"All that is necessary for the triumph of evil
is that good men do nothing." —Edmund Burke

INJUSTICE IS A NOUN. Justice is an active verb. My college English professor would take issue with that statement, but I stand by it. Injustice exists. Until sin is fully conquered with the establishment of Christ's coming kingdom, there will be injustice. We need to study injustice. We need to educate ourselves about injustice.

Justice is an action verb. Justice must not be pronounced "just is." Justice requires action. Justice demands involvement. Justice must not be something that just is. Justice cannot be complacent. "At that time I will search Jerusalem with lamps and punish those who are complacent, who are like wine left on its dregs, who think, 'The Lord will do nothing, either good or bad'" (Zephaniah 1:12). God does not do nothing. He acts in justice. He desires the same of us. This is the lesson from the priest.

The priests were respected leaders who represented both the church and the law. They studied justice in the law and were charged with its application. "In any dispute, the priests are to serve as judges and decide it according to my ordinances. They are to keep my laws and my decrees for all my appointed feasts, and they are to keep my Sabbaths holy" (Ezekiel 44:24). The lawyer to whom Jesus told the story would have identified with the priest. I think we can also.

Luke begins his gospel with the story of a priest named Zechariah. Like most priests, Zechariah was a good man. But he and his wife could not have children. I can relate. And I think we can all relate to how routine Zechariah's life had become.

The priests would take regular business trips. They were part of a division that would travel to Jerusalem to work in the temple for several weeks, then return home.[1] On this occasion Zechariah was chosen by lot to go into the temple and burn incense. That would be a good day at the office. But it is amazing how easy it is to get so involved in routine that we are not prepared to deal with unexpected divine opportunity. For Zechariah, that was an encounter with the angel Gabriel.

Devoutly religious, Zechariah had prayed for an encounter with the divine so he and his wife could have children—and now an angel appeared to tell him he would have a son.

Wouldn't you be excited? Don't be too sure.

Like Zechariah, I was overwhelmed by my encounter with God through the message of His rainbows and His call to serve the least of these. Zechariah was afraid and he doubted. "How can I be sure of this?" he asked.

Do you ever ask yourself that? Are you praying for something more? If so, then the lesson of the priest is yours.

Zechariah's encounter left him speechless—literally. But he was transformed. His son was John the Baptist, who prepared the way of the Lord. Zechariah's song at the end of Luke 1 is a beautiful tribute to God's plan of redemption through salvation "to rescue us from the hands of our enemies, and to enable us to serve him without fear in holiness and righteousness before him all our days" (Luke 1:74–75).

God replaced Zechariah's fear with a song of joy. God has a plan for your life. He provides divine encounters that invade our routine. Will we dare to take action? Or will we question God and miss the opportunity? That is the story of the priest.

The priest in Jesus' story had completed his duties at the temple and was returning home. Maybe, like Zechariah, he had been chosen to burn incense before the Lord. Maybe he was thinking about his service or about getting home to a wonderful meal and seeing his wife and children.

We don't know. But we do know the story provides him—and by extension the church—with an unexpected opportunity. Jesus' story emphasizes the chance meeting of the priest with the injured man.

Jesus, as the creator of the story, knows it is no coincidence that a priest entered the story. Jesus intentionally brings a good man and church leader in contact with evil and injustice. To us, and the priest, the event is unexpected. The priest did not anticipate encountering the injured man. But it was no accident.

All of life is history—His story. Jesus is the creator of all things. Nothing in life happens by chance. As we and the church travel the crooked roads of life, it is no accident that we encounter unexpected opportunities to serve the injured. The difference between our life and the priest in the parable is not chance, but choice.

The priest was purely story and could have no choice—the storyteller made the choice to make a point. But in God's sovereign story, He allows us choice. He knows what we will choose, but He gives us the opportunity.

But if serving the Lord seems undesirable to you, then choose for yourselves this day whom you will serve, whether the gods your forefathers served beyond the River, or the gods of the Amorites, in whose land you are living. But as for me and my household, we will serve the Lord. (Joshua 24:15)

God desires that we choose to love Him, and when we do, His love will so flow into us that we will love our neighbor. But it begins with a choice.

You are not reading this book by chance. The Spirit has a plan for your life. Jesus loves you and wants much more for you. He wants you to experience how wide, deep, and full His love is for you. Like the apostle Paul:

> My response is to get down on my knees before the Father, this magnificent Father who parcels out all heaven and earth. I ask him to strengthen you by his Spirit—not a brute strength but a glorious inner strength—that Christ will live in you as you open the door and invite him in. And I ask him that with both feet planted firmly on love, you'll be able to take in with all followers of Jesus the extravagant dimensions of Christ's love. Reach out and experience the breadth! Test its length! Plumb the depths! Rise to the heights! Live full lives, full in the fullness of God.
>
> God can do anything, you know—far more than you could ever imagine or guess or request in your wildest dreams! He does it not by pushing us around but by working within us, his Spirit deeply and gently within us. (Ephesians 3:14–20 THE MESSAGE)

So what prevents you from experiencing the fullness of God's plan for your life? What stopped the priest? We don't know. But we do know it wasn't by chance that he encountered the injured man. The priest had a divine opportunity. He saw the injured man—but crossed to the other side and walked on.

We can all identify with missed opportunities. Life is so full of stuff that we lose sight of what God wants from us—even when it's right in front of us. Our lives become routine, and we march through each day the same as the last—without deeper meaning and fulfillment. To rediscover purpose, we can learn from the priest.

Priests studied words for their meaning. To examine the meaning of life, why not look at the word itself? Why not look to the heart of the word?

In the middle of the word *life* is the word *if*. That seems appropriate. Life is full of *ifs*. We often worry about the "what ifs" of life, yet no amount of worrying will change the outcome.

Then there are the "if onlys" of life. If only this were to happen, things would be different. Yet those circumstances lie outside our control.

The priest in the parable may have been preoccupied with such thoughts. These questions and regrets can be hidden robbers, stealing the joy from your life and filling it with doubt and regret.

A popular 1970s song by Harry Chapin, "Cat's in the Cradle," exemplifies the regret that comes with missed opportunity. In the song a man is too busy with life and work to pay attention to his son, who grows up to be just like his father. Missed opportunities. We can feel overwhelmed by our lives. So we look at all the needs around us and conclude there are too many—and do nothing.

The needs of the many can be overwhelming, but the lesson of the priest is that it begins with one. We serve one person at a time. We dare not become complacent. We dare not do nothing.

Each moment is a precious gift. Sometimes we mistakenly think we must choose between serving and family. We think of serving as something we do alone. That's a mistake. I'm blessed to serve the injured with my family. My wife, Helen, is bilingual and volunteers in our front office and at events by translating and in many other ways. My sons, Joseph and Daniel, also volunteer. They come into the office and help move furniture, prepare mailings, and serve cookies (and help themselves along the way). Every night they pray for the people coming to our office and that we will have the resources to continue serving more people.

My father and mother live two hours away, but they travel twice a month to volunteer. As a retired pastor, my father works with supporting churches. As a retired social worker, my mother helps train volunteers, answers phones, and encourages others. Serving the injured provides excellent opportunity to set an example. I pray that my boys may grow up to follow me as I follow Christ (1 Corinthians 11:1).

We need to make the most of every opportunity. But as we do, we need to guard our hearts so we can avoid life's extremes.

On one side of the *IF* of life is the letter *I*. If we believe life has no meaning, we can believe that "I must make of life what I choose." We can trust our own strength, beauty, intelligence, or abilities and believe all that matters is *I*. That *I* stands for idol as we place our plans ahead of God's. Few of us do this willfully, but the stuff of life so ensnares us, we miss the opportunities God sends our way.

We have no reason to believe the priest was not a good man. He may have been so preoccupied with thoughts of returning home after several weeks that he "saw" the injured man but didn't really see him.

Have you ever been so focused on something that you completely missed what your spouse, child, or someone else said? You "see," but don't really see what else is around you.

Maybe as he saw the injured man he thought, *I wish I had time to help. I see the need but don't have the time. In a few years that will be different and then I can help.*

All these reasons are good, but they are not godly. "'Why do you call me good?' Jesus answered. 'No one is good—except God alone'" (Luke 18:19). What we perceive as good is often self-focused and not Savior-focused. We justify instead of doing justice.

The priest in the parable was without excuse in not stopping to care for his injured neighbor. The priest who served God, in effect put himself in the place of God and thought he could best use his time and energy by walking past the injured man.

But it is not our life or our time. It all belongs to God. "Now listen, you who say, 'Today or tomorrow we will go to this or that city, spend a year there, carry on business and make money.' Why, you do not even know what will happen tomorrow. What is your life? You are a mist that appears for a little while and then vanishes. Instead, you ought to say, 'If it is the Lord's will, we will live and do this or that.' As it is, you boast and brag. All such boasting is evil" (James 4:13–16).

That is a different way of looking at the *ifs* of life—considering if it is the Lord's will, although focusing on this too much can lead to the other extreme.

On the other side of *IF* is the letter *F*. We all know what an F means. Failure. If everything is predetermined by God, then it doesn't matter what I do, so I'll do nothing. I'm not good enough anyway, so why try?

When I taught business law, I gave Fs to a number of students, but never because that work was the best a student could do. It was always due to a lack of effort.

The times we don't care often arise because of fear and worry. Jesus addressed this issue in His Sermon on the Mount:

> Do not worry about your life, what you will eat or drink; or about your body, what you will wear. Is not life more important than food, and the body more important than

clothes? . . .Who of you by worrying can add a single hour to his life? . . . Therefore do not worry about tomorrow, for tomorrow will worry about itself. Each day has enough troubles of its own. (Matthew 6:25, 27, 34)

The priest may have been afraid. *What if the robbers are still around? I might get hurt and then I wouldn't be able to serve at the temple.*

He might have been afraid that he didn't have the skills to help. He was used to sacrificing living things, not saving them.

The injured man needs someone better qualified than me to help him. I'm sure someone else will help.

GOD DOES NOT CALL THE QUALIFIED; HE QUALIFIES THE CALLED.

The real failure in these thoughts is that we fail to recognize the situation is not about us, but about God. God does not call the qualified; He qualifies the called. If you have the breath of life within you, you can make a difference.

Jesus makes this clear in His choice of twelve ordinary men to serve as His disciples. None was highly qualified to change the world. But they did.

So can you. If life is to have meaning, it must be more than just *I* or *F*. Pride and fear don't bring meaning to life. We must examine *LIFE* more closely. What lies between *I* and *F*? Nothing.

For a person who struggles with *I*, this is a good place to begin to find meaning. As Paul wrote, "Do not think of yourself more highly than you ought, but rather think of yourself with sober judgment, in accordance with the measure of faith God has given you" (Romans 12:3).

For the person who struggles with *F*, the unseen is a good

place to begin to find meaning. As the writer of Hebrews said, "Now faith is being sure of what we hope for and certain of what we do not see" (Hebrews 11:1).

In the midst of life's uncertainties, the only true certainty is a humble faith. In this way the men and women of faith listed in Hebrews 11 were able to face struggles and uncertainty with perseverance and a peace that surpasses understanding.

Do you believe you can experience that type of faith? Or are you like the priest Zechariah asking, "How can I be sure of this?" (Luke 1:18). God's promises are real. His Word is true. You can be empowered to make a difference. But doing so requires choice. And choice requires action. Don't just do life, live life. Let's examine that word. At the heart of *live*—is *IV*. You need to be hooked up to an IV.

You cannot find meaning in life in yourself. You will quickly dehydrate. Since sin entered the world, we live in a dry, weary wasteland. You've felt that. You've longed for something else—for refreshment of your soul. You need to be rehydrated with an IV.

But God will not insert that IV into you without your consent. You have to acknowledge your need. You have to recognize that all your planning could be for nothing, all your worrying and fear brings you no joy. In humility and by faith, you have to recognize your need for a Savior. Jesus Christ created you and believes you have infinite value. He died for you.

Do you believe He is God in flesh, sent to pay the penalty for your pride in trying to do things your own way? Do you believe He loves you and died for you? Do you believe He rose from the dead and wishes to provide you with everlasting, meaningful life? Jesus said, "I have come that they may have life, and have it to the full" (John 10:10). If you want that full, meaningful life, you only have to ask.

Jesus, I've messed up. I've tried to do things my way, and it hasn't worked. I believe You are the Son of God and want to have a relationship with me. Thank You for dying for me. Please enter my heart and my life and change me. I want to live the full, meaningful life You desire for me. Thank You for saving me and setting me free.

If you just prayed that prayer for yourself, welcome to the kingdom—the kingdom of God, where righteousness and justice are the foundation of His throne (Psalm 89:14).

Maybe you were already saved, but the deceitfulness of wealth or the worries of this world have choked your life and you are not experiencing peace or joy. There is help and hope. The history of the world is all about God restoring man unto Himself. For you to live differently, you need to be restored. God has an IV for you.

God's spiritual IV contains medicines for your soul. First is the Spirit. When you accept Christ as Lord of your life, He promises to send His Spirit to comfort, counsel, and convict you. He promised us that "in this world you will have trouble. But take heart! I have overcome the world" (John 16:33).

None of us should be surprised by trouble. Yet Jesus said He was the vine and we were branches, and that if we remained in Him, we would have a fruitful life. But, "apart from me you can do nothing" (John 15:5). So how do we do that?

First, by receiving the Spirit, who convicts us of sin and guides us in truth. But the only way to know this truth is through the second ingredient of our IV: Scripture. The Bible is truth. "All Scripture is God-breathed and is useful for teaching, rebuking, correcting and training in righteousness, so that the man of God may be thoroughly equipped for every good work" (2 Timothy 3:16–17).

Don't you want to be thoroughly equipped for life? You can be. As you regularly read the Bible, the Spirit will guide you and help you put off your old self and put on new ways of living. You will begin to replace old attitudes of anger, bitterness, jealousy, lust, slander, and others with love, joy, peace, patience, kindness, goodness, faithfulness, gentleness, and self-control—the fruits of the Spirit (Galatians 5:22–23).

You need help in doing this. That is why you must seek others and you must serve others. In seeking mature Christians, you learn from them in practical, supportive ways. But don't just seek others—serve others. The Bible is filled with passages about how we are to love one another, serve one another, put the interest of others ahead of our own, and demonstrate mercy and compassion in all we do. In seeking and serving others, you will find a more abundant, meaningful life.

Finally, you need to pray. No greater power exists. It heals, restores, empowers, and provides a lifeline to the life giver. Prayer is how we communicate with God.

Pray without ceasing that you may be filled with the power of the Holy Spirit to accomplish works of service prepared for you from the foundation of the world (see Ephesians 2:10). Opportunities prepared for you. Don't pass them by.

Take the time to stop and help the injured. Bill did. So did Jane.

Loretta was an older widow. Her husband died without a will, and only his name was on their home. Left without sufficient resources, Loretta didn't know what to do. An agency referred her to us for budget counseling.

Bill is retired, but he regularly volunteers as a budget counselor. When he met with Loretta, he realized she needed more monthly cash and suggested a reverse mortgage, since she had no revenue source outside of Social Security, and her only asset was her home. When Bill learned the home was not in Loretta's name, we asked Jane to help.

Jane is a busy attorney, but she chose to stop to help the injured.

Jane filed an estate, published notices, and did what was needed to transfer the home and resolve other outstanding issues. As a result, Loretta was able to stay in her home and work with Bill to establish a budget. But most of all, she found a neighbor in Jane who took time to visit her, talk with her on the phone, pray with her, and let her know God cared for her. "Thank you for praying and understanding," she said.

Life is full of uncertainties. But with a steady diet of the fruits of the Spirit, the meat of the Bible, the fellowship of Christian friends, and regular prayer, we can experience peace. We will be empowered by the Holy Spirit to live differently. We will serve others, and our life will be characterized by a humble faith.

The choice is yours. Will you take the time to serve the injured?

LESSON FROM HISTORY

The final lesson of the priest is a lesson from history. Collectively we as Christians have failed the injured. The church has largely failed to administer justice.

For centuries the church was the primary force behind education and health care in this country. While both institutions have sometimes wandered from these roots, the actions of concerned Christians have made a profound impact. But the church has largely been absent in administering justice for the poor. This is particularly unfortunate given the foundations of law and justice in a biblical worldview.

Lawyer and theologian Udo Middelmann, president of the Francis A. Schaeffer Foundation, notes:

> The rule of law—known to the Jews, imposed on England in the Magna Carta, and later exhibited in the Bill of Rights and similar documents—was only ever labored for in cultures influenced by Judaism and Christianity. The

dominion over creation, a rational approach to the workings of nature, and a moral distinction between what is and what should be all came from the biblical worldview.[2]

The Magna Carta of 1215 first proclaimed the rule of law: "To no man will we sell, or deny, or delay, right or justice."[3] That justice embodied the concept of natural law and moral authority derived from the laws of nature and of nature's God. The goal of all our legal institutions was to secure justice.

These ideas formed the basis of America's law and government. The moral foundation of truth in law enabled our systems to eventually address the horrors of slavery. Our laws freed children from workhouses, gave women the right to vote, and brought about more equality through the Civil Rights Act.

The challenge for America has not been our system of justice, but access to that system. In such circumstances, "the system not only robs the poor of their only protection, but it places in the hands of their oppressors the most powerful and ruthless weapon ever invented. The law itself becomes the means of extortion."[4]

Until the Civil War, America thrived as primarily an agricultural society. Lawyers worked with local communities and when payment could not be made, some form of barter was easily established.

But with the rise of cities and larger populations came abuses and an inability by the poor to access justice. Jacob Riis brought this to light in 1890 through his work, *How the Other Half Lives*.[5] This led to tenement reforms and was a major impetus in the first great study of the problem of injustice among the poor. That study by Reginald Heber Smith in 1919 concluded: "The administration of American justice is not impartial, the rich and the poor do not stand on an equality before the law, the traditional method of providing justice has operated to close the doors of the courts to the poor, and has caused a gross denial of justice in all parts of the country to millions of persons."[6]

Legal Aid began in 1876, when a group of twenty German merchants in New York City took action. They were outraged by the treatment of German immigrants being taken advantage of in housing, contracts, and employment because they did not know English. These businessmen pooled their resources and hired an advocate who became the nation's first legal-aid attorney, serving hundreds of poor immigrants who could not afford one.

That organization was limited in scope.[7] In 1888 the first true legal aid organization began in Chicago—the Bureau of Justice.[8] This organization was supported by donations and served all people of low-income, regardless of nationality, race, or sex. The early legal aid societies struggled with inadequate funding. "During its early years, legal aid reached less than 1 percent of those in need. Many areas of the country had no legal aid at all, and those legal aid programs that did exist were woefully underfunded."[9]

By the end of World War I, only forty-one legal-aid organizations existed.[10] The Great Depression expanded the need for services, but with no unifying force and no funding, the growth in providing justice for the poor was small.

In the wake of the civil rights movement and with the advent of welfare, the government sought involvement in 1965 through the Office of Economic Opportunity Legal Services.

A key to ensuring the influence of the organized bar was the agreement to create a National Advisory Committee, which included leaders of the bar, along with client representatives and others knowledgeable about civil legal assistance. The National Advisory Committee included a number of people who were to play critical roles in the future of the federal legal services program, including John Robb, a private attorney in Albuquerque, New Mexico.[11]

John Robb would spend the next forty-five years as one of the nation's leading advocates for legal aid and Christian Legal Aid. In 2006 the American Bar Association recognized John as the first individual to receive their highest life achievement award for being a "Distinguished Lawyer and Advocate for Low-Income Individuals and Families, for Life Demonstrated Commitment to 'Equal Justice for All.'"

While the nation's first experiment with federal legal assistance was facing challenges, Christian Legal Aid quietly began in 1973. That same year, Congress began dismantling the Office of Economic Opportunity Legal Services, which was replaced in 1974 with the federal Legal Services Corporation, which remains the primary secular funding source for legal aid.[12]

In the shadow of the nation's first true legal aid program in Chicago, Bill Leslie, pastor of LaSalle Street Church, saw the need in his community of Cabrini Green for a Christian legal-aid program. He spoke to a young attorney named Chuck Hogren.

Chuck told Bill if he could raise the first year's expenses, he would lead this new program. Two months later the church had raised the funds, and three months later, on February 1, 1973, Cabrini Green Legal Aid opened its doors.[13] This partnership between the church and justice for the poor is an important model, which we will examine more in Chapter 8. The church and individual Christians have a vital role to play in justice ministry.

For nearly two hundred years, the church in America was largely silent on justice for the poor. Like the priest, we walked past the injured. The church formed many wonderful service ministries, but did little to administer justice using the law. We saw the need but crossed to the other side.

Bill Leslie and Chuck Hogren were among the first Samaritans to stop. They have been followed by some churches, other individuals,[14] and Christian Legal Aid organizations.[15] The first effort on a national level was led by John Robb and the Christian Legal Society (CLS), who recognized the significantly incomplete work of the government in providing legal aid to the poor. As John Robb wrote:

Why is it that nearly all funding for legal aid for the poor came from government sources, volunteer services of bar associations, and lawyers serving in pro bono programs who served primarily from a sense of professional responsibility? Didn't the Bible have something to say about obligations for Christians and the Christian Church to help the poor? Did God have a definite part to play in legal aid?[16]

John Robb and his colleagues believed God desired justice for the poor, and that Christian Legal Aid uniquely answered God's call to "defend the rights of the poor and needy" (Proverbs 31:9). In the early 1980s he was involved in the Christian Legal Aid and Referral Service in Albuquerque, which later became the New Mexico Christian Legal Aid Program. The latter grew out of meetings John had with the Christian Legal Society to launch a national effort to encourage the creation of Christian Legal Aid organizations. At the same time, Robb volunteered to become the first national director of public ministries with CLS.

Robb created materials and traveled across the country to encourage attorneys to get involved in Christian Legal Aid. One of the early CLS legal-aid conferences was held in San Antonio, Texas. A young, successful attorney listened.

That attorney spoke afterward with Robb and Hogren. As he

toured the Alamo, where courageous men had stood against impossible odds, he knew the Bible was filled with such men. Would he have the courage to launch a new organization? Would he look at his circumstances, with a wife staying home and newborn twins, and pass the opportunity by? He did not.

I began Administer Justice four months later. The fledgling ministry would lead this new wave of Christian Legal Aid, where gospel justice for the poor was the guiding principle. Others joined and became a loose consortium encompassing sixty-two local, independent programs in twenty-five states and the District of Columbia, and four in Africa. This "network" in 2009 provided help to approximately 30,000 clients directly, and an estimated 250,000 people in their immediate and extended families.[17]

With no strong, unifying structure for support, and with a lack of funds, by 2011 this group dwindled to forty-seven. Recognizing the need for a new national initiative, John Robb and I met with other leaders to form Gospel Justice Initiative to excite and equip churches, attorneys, and individuals to defend the rights of the poor and needy through legal help and gospel hope.

While the past demonstrates some missed opportunity, God offers second chances. The present provides unparalleled opportunity for churches, Christians, and Christian attorneys to make a difference through gospel justice. The future will be determined by the choices we make today.

Will we seize this opportunity? Will we incorporate a vital ministry to serve the injured man—or will we cross to the other side of the road? May we make the most of this opportunity, for the days are evil and injustice abounds.

The priest had a choice. By his inaction he chose injustice. Now the choice is ours.

CHAPTER 5

LESSONS FROM THE LEVITE

"Then a Levite religious man showed up; he also avoided
the injured man." —Luke 10:32 THE MESSAGE

"They sow the wind and reap the whirlwind." —Hosea 8:7

SHE CAME CAUTIOUS and alone. She felt ostracized
among her own and was wary of outsiders. Distrustful and abra-
sive, she'd seen five marriages dissolve. Now she had a live-in boyfriend. With such a history, should anyone offer her help?

Doesn't justice mean getting one's just deserts from bad decisions? *She's obviously made a series of bad choices; now she needs to live
with the consequences. It would be wrong to offer aid and support such a
sinful lifestyle. She's obviously turned her back on God, and He is punish-
ing her for her sin.* Those could have been the thoughts of the Levite.

The Levites were deeply religious. They alone of the tribes of
Israel were set apart for special service and devotion to God. They
knew the law and served as judges. King Jehoshaphat appointed the
Levites "to administer the law of the Lord and to settle disputes"
(2 Chronicles 19:8). The Levites took this responsibility seriously.

While the Levite was part of the legal system, he represents
more broadly all those who observe the laws of God and man.
Today many Christians hesitate to offer aid to those who have
willfully violated those laws.

▶ It only seems fair that they suffer.
▶ They should be warned not to sin against the Lord.

▸ They should be told to obey the authorities.

▸ For us to help would be abetting their sin.

▸ We should avoid them and allow God to judge them.

▸ If God is judging them, who are we to intervene?

In the parable, the Levite could well have had such thoughts. *This man was obviously not careful. Now look at him. How unfortunate. But there must be a reason for his suffering. May God's will be done.* And he chose to walk past.

Or maybe the Levite thought, *God has commanded me to stay away from a dead body,*[1] *and I must not take God's word lightly. If I begin to help this man and he dies, I will defile myself. I must not stain myself with this man's sin.*

I have a good Christian friend who told me, "I have an intense sense of justice." He volunteered with us, but after encountering individuals like the woman at the beginning of this chapter, he would shake his head. "They sow the wind and reap the whirlwind," he would say. "Whenever I come here, I feel like I'm wading in a cesspool."

Others refer to our waiting room as a triage center. Yes, those who come are broken and bleeding from the effects of a sinful world. Sin is ugly. Brokenness is messy. But by focusing on the dirt and blood of the broken, we become the Levite.

After many discussions with my friend, I had to ask him to stop volunteering. Justice without mercy is harsh and legalistic. "He who mocks the poor shows contempt for their Maker; whoever gloats over disaster will not go unpunished" (Proverbs 17:5).

The Levite believes in punishment of sin—that justice means getting what one deserves. The Levite believes he has special insight from God, lives a pure life, and is blessed. Those in trouble, ensnared by sin, are suffering the just consequences.

But the Levite is wrong. "Men at ease have contempt for misfortune as the fate of those whose feet are slipping" (Job 12:5). The lesson of the parable is that the Levite was without excuse. While we might applaud the Levite, Jesus was showing us he'd missed an opportunity to serve his neighbor.

The Levites and religious leaders frequently criticized Jesus for spending time with sinners: "Here is a glutton and a drunkard, a friend of tax collectors and 'sinners,'" they would say, but Jesus said, "wisdom is proved right by her actions" (Matthew 11:19). The action of stopping, getting in the dirt, and caring for the injured.

> ARE WE SO DIFFERENT FROM THE LEVITE? THE DISCIPLES WEREN'T.

Are we so different from the Levite? The disciples weren't. More than once they expected retribution. "Rabbi, who sinned, this man or his parents, that he was born blind?" (John 9:2). When some Samaritans did not welcome Jesus, James and John asked, "Lord, do you want us to call fire down from heaven to destroy them?" (Luke 9:54). They didn't flinch when teachers of the law brought a woman caught in adultery to Jesus to see justice served (John 8:3–4).

Each time, someone wanted justice to be punishment. Good religious people believed the person should get what was coming. They wanted validation of their view of justice. Instead they received rebuke (Luke 9:55).

Concerning the man born blind, Jesus explained, "Neither this man nor his parents sinned. . . . this happened so that the work of God might be displayed in his life" (John 9:3).

And what of the woman who so clearly violated the law? The law said, "You must purge the evil from Israel," by stoning the woman (Deuteronomy 22:22).

Jesus strongly disagrees with those who believe in just deserts. He not only warned against a heart of judgment, but He also demonstrated what it meant to show mercy. Jesus reminded those in authority that they were sinners. He restored the woman to a new life and told her to leave her life of sin.[2]

In John 9, Jesus had mercy on the man born blind. But He incurred the judgment of the teachers of the law by healing the man on the Sabbath. The Levites criticized Jesus as a sinful lawbreaker. The Sabbath law was clear and Jesus violated it. Jesus should be punished. All who violate the law should be punished.

But the man born blind could see things more clearly. "Whether he is a sinner or not, I don't know," he said. "One thing I do know. I was blind, but now I see!" (John 9:25).

Jesus never excused or ignored sin—and neither should we. But He demonstrated the importance of mercy. Nowhere is that more evident than in His unjust death on our behalf. We deserve retribution. We deserve punishment. But Jesus demonstrated mercy. He brought forgiveness and grace by taking our sin upon Himself. So how can we act like the Levite?

What would you have done if you encountered the woman at the beginning of this chapter—a racial and social outcast steeped in sin?

The Levite would say she is getting what she deserves and walk on by. Jesus stopped.

The woman was a Samaritan coming to a well in the middle of the day because she was an outcast. No other Jewish man would have dared to speak to her. But Jesus took the opportunity to meet her where she was. She needed water, and He provided living water. She needed hope, and He showed her the Messiah. A brief encounter changed her life and the lives of many in her village.[3]

The disciples would have avoided Samaria. They preferred to call down fire from heaven on the Samaritans. But Jesus demonstrated true justice: a gospel justice that neither ignores sin, nor the people caught in its effects.

"Be wise in the way you act toward outsiders; make the most of every opportunity" (Colossians 4:5). The Levite thought he was wise, but he missed an opportunity. He thought he was right to judge and walk on by his neighbor in need, but, "there is only one Lawgiver and Judge, the one who is able to save and destroy. But you—who are you to judge your neighbor?" (James 4:12).

Rather we ought to "speak and act as those who are going to be judged by the law that gives freedom, because judgment without mercy will be shown to anyone who has not been merciful. Mercy triumphs over judgment!" (James 2:12–13).

The Levite forgot why God gave him no allotment of land. The Levite was to live by faith on the provision of others "so that the Levites (who have no allotment or inheritance of their own) and the aliens, the fatherless and the widows who live in your towns may come and eat and be satisfied, and so that the Lord your God may bless you in all the works of your hands" (Deuteronomy 14:29).

The Levite was to live like the widow, the fatherless, the alien, and the poor.[4] He was to praise God as his provider —and not rely on his superior knowledge or position to stand in judgment over the very people he was called to identify with. "You should not look down on your brother in the day of his misfortune, nor rejoice over the people of Judah in the day of their destruction, nor boast so much in the day of their trouble" (Obadiah 1:12).

The lesson of the Levite is a constant challenge for the church, the Christian, and for the Christian lawyer. It is for me.

I understand the Levite well. I must constantly check my heart or that's who I become. The son of a pastor, I've never smoked or drank, I've never taken drugs, I don't swear, and I've known only one woman. I attended a Christian college and a top-ranked law school and served as an elder and pastor. I've read and committed much of the Bible to memory.

I was Saul. He was also a lawyer with a good resume who thought he had the right to judge others. I believed it would not be fair for God to treat a murderer, an adulterer, a divorced person, or an illegal immigrant the same as me. They deserve to be punished for their sin. Likewise, Saul believed, this new group calling themselves "the Way" should be punished for violating the law. The law exists to restrain sin, and sinners should be punished under the law.

I was Jonah, the prophet who thought the people of Nineveh should be punished for their sin. I believed people who choose to have too many kids and not work deserved their fate. In America opportunity abounds, and if they choose not to succeed, then I'm not going to help them. Like Jonah, I didn't like the idea that the Lord "is gracious and compassionate, slow to anger and rich in love. The Lord is good to all; he has compassion on all he has made" (Psalm 145:8–9).

I liked truth and justice, not compassion and love. As a Levite I forgot my roots, that I was a sinner saved by grace. I looked at justice from man's perspective, and I looked pretty good. But from God's perspective I was proud and arrogant. I was unconcerned with the needs of others.

AS A LEVITE I FORGOT MY ROOTS, THAT I WAS A SINNER SAVED BY GRACE.

By God's grace I was Jonah, and God sent storms into my life. In God's mercy I was Saul, and He provided a Damascus road moment where I heard His voice.

I now weep over the lost opportunities I walked past. Like Paul I realize I am the worst of sinners, but I thank God for His mercy (see 1 Timothy 1:15–16). Paul learned his lessons from a Levite, and I began to see why.

Paul's teacher was Barnabas who was born Joseph, a Levite from Cyprus.[5] His name was changed because he was a "son of encouragement." When others judged Paul and would have nothing to do with him, Barnabas intervened.

Earlier when the church was in need, Barnabas had sold his possessions, and given his money, his time, and his energy to aid others. God desires Levites like Barnabas who do not seek their own good, but that of others.[6]

May God make us like Barnabas with open hearts and open eyes to see the needs of the injured.[7] Those needs are all around us. We have great opportunity to look, to stop, and to bring mercy and compassion to the injured.

The call to serve the injured is a call to get messy. Perhaps there is no messier area than the issues of broken families: difficulties between husband and wife, between parent and child, illegitimacy, delinquency, guardianship, custody, and adoption. They involve the security of the home and the welfare of children.

Most cases across the country served by legal aid organizations involve these family issues.[8] They are too important to ignore. And they pervade the church and Christian families.

The church is to be applauded for establishing divorce recovery programs, but we have missed an opportunity. Preventative education is becoming more prevalent and should be expanded. Many injured need more. They need someone to get involved in the messiness of marriage.

The church can lead the way. Administer Justice trains individuals and attorneys through Peacemaker Ministries[9] in delivering conciliation services to reconcile and restore that which is broken.

As Ken Sande, the founder of Peacemaker Ministries writes,

"God delights to work in us and through us as we rely on His promises to obey His commands for peacemaking. At the same time, He is deeply committed to helping us understand the root causes of our conflicts and changing the attitudes and habits that threaten our relationships. In short, God is eager to display the wonders of the gospel in the midst of our marital and family conflicts so that He can reveal the life-changing power of His Son, Jesus Christ."[10]

The church had given up on Karl and Debbie. Counseling, classes, and meetings with leadership had not changed the constant fighting in the home. The church did not have the time or the resources to engage any further in what appeared to be hard hearts and a hopeless cause. They would become yet another divorce statistic. Then the court system referred them to us.

Karl said their marital problems were psychological—his wife was "psycho" and he was "logical." Debbie painted a very different picture: He was angry and controlling, but she was always right. Their three young children were caught in the middle.

Our office assigns a trained male and female team to each mediation. The women meet separately, as do the men, before coming together to lay a foundation of hope.

When couples come to us, hope is almost always gone. Our first question is always, "Do you believe Jesus Christ died for you to set you free from sin?" If so, then there is hope. The second question is, "Do you believe that with God all things are possible?" If so, then there is hope. It takes a small view of God not to believe He can transform hearts, change lives, and restore marriages.

The only commitment we ask is that the person be open to God's leading. Only the power of the Holy Spirit can change lives. A spouse can't change the other person, and neither can a mediator. But God will not judge a wife for whether she changed her husband. God will judge her for whether her heart was right before Him. The same is true for the husband.

People spend so much time worrying or getting angry over things they cannot control—their work, children, spouse—they forget to spend time on what they can control—the attitudes of their heart, their time spent in the Word and prayer, their relationship with God.

Karl and Debbie reluctantly agreed to meet. It was better than going to court. Each wanted to divide things up between them. But they made a commitment to explore reconciliation—though they believed it impossible.

Their hostility was obvious. While there are specific ground rules, participants often need to be reminded. They want to cut the other person off to correct some perceived injustice. When this happens, our mediators often hand out two large flyswatters—one black and the other blue.

"If you want to lash out at one another and make each other black and blue," they say, "use these." Written on the flyswatters is: "What causes you to swat at one another? Isn't it the desires that battle within you? Read what the Bible says in James 4." That is a great passage on how our desires get in the way of God's desires and how we must humble ourselves so He can lift us up.

Mediation takes time. But if individuals are willing to seek God with the help of trained volunteer mediators, change can take place. Today Karl and Debbie are fully reconciled. Every year the family photo shows three growing children smiling with their mom and dad. Both parents are active in ministry, and Karl has trained to serve others as a mediator.

Couples who complete their mediation are assigned a mature couple from a local church to walk alongside them for one year.

We in the church need not pass by the messy problems families face. We need to avoid the lies of the world that have become marriage robbers along the Jericho Road.

The breakdown of families is destroying our churches, communities, and country. We need to pray against the forces that attack families from every side. And we need to fight for marriage. While the goal should be restoration and reconciliation whenever possible, sometimes that does not happen. We must guard against judging our neighbors experiencing divorce and numerous other family problems.

Not every parent of a wayward child is being punished for being a bad parent. Children make choices. Not every wayward husband or wife is reacting against a bad partner. Spouses make choices.

This is a lesson I learned from Tina, a wonderful young mother who one day woke up to a shattered, completely unexpected world. Here is her story in her own words.

TINA'S STORY

This week as I was walking down the hall at my new job, I thought, *this is how a miracle feels.* I remembered being without a job—yet with a mortgage; without a husband in my house—yet with a husband; and without money to care for my son. My life now is nothing short of a miracle, and Administer Justice is a tool God used to make a huge difference in my life.

In 2005, my high school sweetheart and husband, the father of my son, left us. A man who had once followed after God's own heart lost his way in such a devastating and profound way, he no longer felt he could be a part of our family. He felt he needed a divorce. I felt split open, left carrying my entrails in my hands. One night while I tried to comfort our three-year-old son to sleep, he said, "Mom, I want my old life back."

We both did. I believe even my wandering, hurting husband wanted that.

With divorce paperwork pending, I sought legal advice. My

parents gave me funds to visit several attorneys who explained we had a strong case—we could "annihilate" and seek hidden funds if there were any. At the very least we could "humiliate." They felt he needed to pay for the pain he was inflicting on us.

Taking their advice would have led us to revenge, anger, and the illusion that this would cause a "win." The attorneys told me I deserved retribution. I wanted reconciliation.

I desperately needed encouragement to pursue forgiveness and compassion while still protecting my son so we would have food and shelter. I was a college-educated stay-at-home mother with no money in the bank. I had to borrow money for gas from my parents to get to the Administer Justice appointment.

Even in my broken and pained state, I knew I needed practical help—to sort out how I was going to put food on the table and pay the mortgage.

People would ask me how I was doing and I wanted to cry out in response, but they didn't really want to know and hurried past me. I felt like a leper who should be crying out "unclean."

I prayed, and my family prayed with me, that the Lord would lead us somewhere where the souls of the clients—the opposing side and the side being represented—mattered the most. A place where legal knowledge was filtered through biblical knowledge. A place where justice did not come at the expense of compassion.

From that first moment walking into the Administer Justice office, I felt God's presence. The volunteers, the woman who greeted me with kindness at the desk—each had a hand in healing my crushed spirit.

I cried as the attorney prayed for me and also for my husband and son. No one shrunk back from me. They wrapped their arms around me. They promised protection through their legal knowledge, yet demonstrated God's healing love.

Through their mediation services and legal expertise, Administer

Justice gave me the strength I needed. They got involved in the mess that sin had racked upon our family; they demonstrated love to all involved. Administer Justice had become the broad place I prayed for in the words of David:

> Be gracious to me, O Lord, for I am in distress; my eye is wasted away from grief, my soul and my body also. For my life is spent with sorrow. (Psalm 31:9–10a NASB)

> You have seen my affliction; You have known the troubles of my soul, and you have not given me over the hand of the enemy; you have set my feet in a large place. (Psalm 31:7–8 NASB)

> I would have despaired unless I had believed that I would see the goodness of the Lord in the land of the living. (Psalm 27:13 NASB)

Finding Administer Justice was an answer to the prayers of my whole family. My husband turned his back on us. But they gave me the opportunity to sit across the table from him and let him know I forgave him. Nothing could separate him from God's love or from mine (Romans 8:39).

On our day in court, I was able to stand before the judge and express God's love for my husband. While our marriage was ending, I could tell the judge I would pray for my husband that one day we might be restored.

That would not happen. Many months later, my husband died. My son and I were truly left alone. I am so grateful I had the chance to look him in the eye and let him know I forgave him for the horrible choices that he made. Those moments of forgiveness, facilitated by Administer Justice, were ones I never would have had, if I had chosen to take to the battlefield instead of the cross.

Years have passed. I have a job and a home. I have my son. I will always carry a broad emotional scar, but I prayerfully realized that maybe God could use me to be that "large place" to someone else, or inspire more to extend the compassion so needed by hurting people in messy situations.

I recently met another single mom at church. She wasn't able to speak through the tears streaming down her face as a friend said this woman's husband had left and she isn't sure what will happen. Her house may be in foreclosure this week, and she went to the food pantry today to make sure she had enough for her two children.

As I hugged her, I told her I have walked in this shadowy place and there will be a day that it will be better. I asked if she knew about Administer Justice and said, "I want you to save up your strength. All you need to do tomorrow is find the strength to call this number. I am confident you will be stronger and more at peace, even if all you need is someone to talk you through the maze of what is happening."

How could I be so confident? I am one who was torn apart and left bleeding, with nowhere to turn, but was rescued through Administer Justice's devotion to a God who believes in defending the weak, comforting those in need, and speaking hope into every dark corner.

Tina reminds us that God is not willing that any should perish. God restores people even when relationships remain broken. "'The Lord will call you back as if you were a wife deserted and distressed in spirit—a wife who married young, only to be rejected,' says your God. 'For a brief moment I abandoned you, but with deep compassion I will bring you back'"(Isaiah 54:6–7).

To my fellow Levite, I ask that we not view the injured as

sowing the wind and reaping the whirlwind. One day we will all stand before God's judgment seat.[11] Until that day comes, let us love God with all our heart, mind, and soul. But let us not miss the opportunity to love our neighbor.

This Sunday you will encounter a Tina caught in the storms of this life. They are walking through the valley of the shadow of death. Will you take the opportunity to stop and serve them? Or will you lift your voice in worship while the one next to you slowly bleeds to death?

Serving our injured neighbor is not easy. It is not comfortable. But it is rewarding. Take the time to not just say you will pray, but actually pray with the person. Then look for places that can provide practical help and seek to partner with them. By doing so you will "sow for yourselves righteousness, reap the fruit of unfailing love, and break up your unplowed ground; for it is time to seek the Lord, until he comes and showers righteousness (justice) on you" (Hosea 10:12).

CHAPTER 6

LESSONS FROM THE SAMARITAN

"Then a despised Samaritan came along, and when he saw
the man, he felt compassion for him." —Luke 10:33 NLT

"This is what the Lord Almighty says: 'Administer true
justice; show mercy and compassion to one another.'"
—Zechariah 7:9

THE SMELL OF CIGARETTES and alcohol entered
the room with her. Hands wringing, Angela looked to Judy for
help as she described her situation. Angela's twelve-year-old son
had died tragically. Her father suffered a stroke, so she was caring
for him. Her small, run-down home had flooded, and now every
time a heavy rain fell, raw sewage would fill her basement and
bathtub.

Angela could not cope. Alcohol numbed the pain, but at the
cost of losing her job. As she continued to spiral downward, she
failed to pay her taxes, her home went into foreclosure, and her
health deteriorated.

Angela cried, drank, smoked, and drifted into despair. The IRS
referred her to our office.

Like many of the poor, Angela had legal problems, financial
problems, tax problems, health problems, and practical problems.
Some of her tragic circumstances were beyond her control, some
the result of poor choices. Angela claimed no faith, but she was a
bleeding neighbor.

After retiring from teaching, Judy pursued law as a second career but was uncertain how to use her law degree. A friend told her about Administer Justice. Judy began volunteering two days a week.

Judy had compassion for Angela. First Judy enlisted additional help. Senior Services provided assistance for Angela's father. The Salvation Army assisted with food. Judy intervened with the IRS on the issue of back taxes, another attorney intervened with the village to fix the sewage problems, and a third attorney intervened in the foreclosure to prevent Angela and her disabled father from becoming homeless.

Knowing Angela had no friends, Judy purchased a gift card for her for Christmas. Angela still does not attend church, and she continues to encounter problems as a result of alcohol, recently landing in jail after drinking and driving.

Angela is a Samaritan. Not the Samaritan of Luke 10, but the one of Luke 17.

That Samaritan was a leper. Everyone avoided lepers, who were required to cry "unclean" and remain outside of town. Messy people like Angela, with their multiple issues, are modern-day lepers. In Luke 17, Jesus chose to stop and heal ten lepers. He told them to present themselves to the priest. Only one leper returned to thank Jesus, and he was a Samaritan.

"Judy, I want to thank you for all you have done for me," Angela wrote. "You and your associates make the world a better place to live in. You gave me hope when all I had was fear and dread. Thank you with all my heart."

People try to avoid these modern-day lepers, whether homeless, alcoholic, or mentally challenged. The courts have established homeless courts and special mental health courts to help these individuals with legal issues. But without access to a lawyer, many are powerless. There is a great opportunity for churches, individuals, and attorneys to partner with a Salvation Army, Union Gospel Mission, or faith-based community ministry in serving our modern-day lepers with legal assistance and education.

Did the leper in Luke 17 accept that Jesus was the Messiah? I don't know. At some point will Angela come to understand the hope of Jesus, or will alcohol consume her life? I don't know.

The lesson of the Samaritan in Luke 10 is that we serve the broken regardless. Jesus said, "Love your enemies, do good to those who hate you, bless those who curse you, pray for those who mistreat you" (Luke 6:27–28). We are called to serve people regardless of their race, religion, or any other status. God's compassion is not conditional.

In Matthew 15, when Jesus provided bread for the four thousand, He did not give it on the condition that they believed He was the Messiah and the Bread of Life. Many rejected His message. If that is true of Jesus, then certainly it will be true for us, as we follow His example in meeting practical needs while providing lasting hope to all: Muslims and Hindus, Asians and Africans, documented and undocumented, skeptics and backsliders.

LESSON ONE: WHO THE SAMARITAN WAS

In Jesus' day, Samaritans and Jews despised each other. They could be the blacks and whites in the U.S. in the 1950s: segregated, distrustful, and full of hatred. The Jews used *Samaritan* in much the same way whites used the "N-word." In John 8:48, the Jewish leaders called Jesus a "Samaritan and demon-possessed." That is the level of hatred which existed between them.

In hearing Jesus' story, the audience would immediately associate the Samaritan with the robbers who attacked the poor Jewish man. To the Jews, Samaritans were not to be trusted.

I have an African-American friend who is a pastor. He describes how when he drives through a more affluent white community, he is often followed by police. He has been stopped for rolling through a stop sign, failing to use a turn signal, and other minor infractions.

Prejudice exists. Most of us, to some degree, judge others based on race, ethnicity, clothing, or other factors. This was certainly true for the Jews and Samaritans.

Samaritans derived their name from Hebrew *Shomerim* meaning "those who observe the law." They believed the Samaritan Torah, which listed Mount Gerizim as the true place of worship, not Jerusalem.[1] They saw themselves as the true followers of the law.

The hatred between the Jews and Samaritans went back to the days of the Assyrian and Babylonian exiles. The Samaritans in the former northern kingdom of Israel not only followed in a tradition that the people of Judah considered apostate; they intermarried with surrounding nations and worshiped their idols (see 2 Kings 17:24–34). When the Jews returned from exile to their land, Ezra cast the Samaritans out of the Jewish assembly. The Samaritans retaliated by sending dispatches to Babylon to stop the rebuilding of Jerusalem.[2] Nehemiah was forced to address the lies of the Samaritans for the rebuilding to take place.[3]

With such history, how could a rabbi tell a story with a Samaritan as hero?

Imagine how shocked the injured Jewish man was. He would never expect mercy and compassion from someone so distrusted. The impact of the Samaritan's identity is hard for us to grasp. We think of a Samaritan, especially a "good Samaritan," in very positive terms.

We even have Good Samaritan laws, to protect those who choose to tend to the injured. The reason such laws are needed is to help bystanders overcome the fear of being sued. Today the Samaritan could be a lawyer.

When America was formed, lawyers were a respected profession. Today lawyers consistently rank in the lowest of professions in Gallup's Honesty and Ethics poll.[4] Like the Samaritans, lawyers are often distrusted and viewed as robbers with excessive fees.

Part of the powerful impact of Administer Justice is the impact of the Samaritan. Imagine you are overwhelmed by the circumstances and choices of life. No one seems to care and everyone passes you by. Then someone stops. They look you in the eye. They pray for you and provide practical help. When that person is a lawyer, it turns your world upside-down.

Stopping to serve is unexpected. When that service is done with compassion and prayer, the effects are significant. Every week we get cards from clients expressing this. "I found myself instructed, calmed, and prayed for," one client wrote. "I feel more able to deal with whatever difficult circumstances may lie ahead. Thank you for your service using your gifts to help people."

> STOPPING TO SERVE IS UNEXPECTED. WHEN THAT SERVICE IS DONE WITH COMPASSION AND PRAYER, THE EFFECTS ARE SIGNIFICANT.

For the first time in many years, Jim walked through the doors of the church. He hadn't found religion; he was losing his home. We have branch offices in churches as we partner to bring justice to a community.

Jim would not have entered a church to see a pastor, but he was there completing papers so he could meet a lawyer. The papers included an optional religious section. One question asks if you believe you will live with God in heaven when you die. Jim hadn't thought about that, but a friend had died that week and he wondered. He marked "uncertain" and hurried to complete the forms so he could get answers to his questions about foreclosure.

A kind woman offered him a cup of coffee as he handed her

the forms. He sat and looked over a rack of legal and spiritual bro-
chures, but was too anxious to grab any. He scanned the room at
huddles of twenty to thirty people completing forms. Men, women,
and children of differing ages and races were being attended by
volunteers. A man called his name, and Jim walked toward him.

"Are you an attorney?"

"No, I'm a volunteer. I teach at Wheaton College and help
here whenever I can." He led Jim to an office where a young man
introduced himself as Bryan and asked Jim to take a seat.

The first thing Bryan said was, "May I pray for you?"

Jim couldn't remember the last time someone prayed for
him—and he was certain he'd never had a lawyer pray for him, but
he consented. The words came but Jim didn't hear them—he felt
them. The compassion was like an overwhelming physical presence. He found himself in tears.

Bryan showed compassion as he listened to Jim's story. He
provided specific guidance concerning the foreclosure, but also encouraged Jim to come to the church and to think about the plan
God had for his life. He gave him some materials from the church.

Jim felt a weight lift from his shoulders.

A couple of days later Jim came to the church for his friend's
funeral. Many people were present, but he was surprised when
Bryan sat behind him. They had both known the young man who
died. That connection led to a series of calls and emails—and an
introduction to one of the pastors. The pastor led Jim to Christ.

Jim is now involved in the church and in a men's group. His
house continues to move along the foreclosure process, but Jim is
no longer overwhelmed that he may lose it. He has gained something more important. He now has a firm answer to the question:
Do you believe you will live with God in heaven when you die?
Whatever happens to his home on earth, he has a home in heaven
that can never be foreclosed.

GOD LOOKS AT THE HEART

The first lesson of the Samaritan in Jesus' parable was his identity. Jesus chose a despised, distrusted person to demonstrate mercy. While anyone could have demonstrated mercy, the story's impact lay in the unexpected.

God does not look at people as we do. Not every Samaritan was the same. Neither is every lawyer. We must not judge others based on externals.

Jesus' audience would have been shocked by the actions of the Samaritan. You may be shocked to know there are hundreds, likely thousands, of attorneys who love their neighbor and stop to serve the injured. Attorneys like Judy, Bryan, and David.

David was a busy attorney, but he believed God had provided him those skills to be an attorney—and that he should share them with the poor. He gladly volunteered four hours on a Saturday morning and appreciated telling his wife and children how he was helping people who had nowhere else to go for help.

One morning as he entered the side door of the church, he prayed for God's guidance. He said hello to the other attorney volunteering that morning and read through the list of clients and issues: family, housing, employment, consumer, Social Security, fraud. The issues were always varied. As a real estate and probate attorney, he felt ill-equipped.

A young woman volunteer handed him the paperwork for his first client. He looked over June's long answers filled with hate for her husband, who was having an affair with her sister. David prayed for guidance and brought June in.

"Hi June, my name is Dave. I'm a volunteer attorney with Administer Justice. It's a Christian organization and if it's okay with you, I'd like to open our time together in prayer."

"Okay," June said curtly.

As Dave prayed, the atmosphere changed and June softened.

Dave listened to June describe her hurt and betrayal. He provided some answers and direction, then stopped.

"June, we've talked about our laws and I know you want justice. You've been abandoned and betrayed. I want you to know there is a God who promises never to leave you or forsake you. He is the only one who can dispense perfect justice in this terrible situation."

Dave talked about God and how all of us will be judged and none found perfect. We all fall short, but God is gracious. He opened his Bible to Isaiah and read:

> The Lord longs to be gracious to you; he rises to show you compassion. For the Lord is a God of justice. Blessed are all who wait for him! . . . How gracious he will be when you cry for help! As soon as he hears, he will answer you. Although the Lord gives you the bread of adversity and the water of affliction, your teachers will be hidden no more; with your own eyes you will see them. Whether you turn to the right or to the left, your ears will hear a voice behind you, saying, "This is the way; walk in it." (Isaiah 30:18–21)

Gently he asked, "Do you want to walk in that way?"

June was weeping. Layers of bitterness and hurt washed from her like the mascara staining her cheeks.

Dave explained the plan of salvation, and June joyfully accepted Christ. She had come to church to meet a lawyer. She left having met her Savior.

LESSON TWO: WHAT THE SAMARITAN DID

Going over to him, the Samaritan soothed his wounds with olive oil and wine and bandaged them. Then he put the man on his own donkey and took him to an inn, where he took care of him. The next day he handed the innkeeper two silver coins, telling him, "Take care of this man. If his bill runs higher than this, I'll pay you the next time I'm here." (Luke 10:34–35 NLT)

The second lesson of the Samaritan is what he did. Christian Buckley and Ryan Dobson make this observation in their book *Humanitarian Jesus:*

> He did something of substance. He didn't pass by like the others. He had compassion that led him to do something. No qualifications, excuses, or expectations of anything in return. He served the man personally and financially— a man who most of his fellow Samaritans would have avoided because of his race, faith, and lifestyle.[5]

The Samaritan chose to overlook the differences between them and soothed the wounds of the injured. He took what he had—olive oil and wine—and ripped his own clothing to make bandages.

But he didn't just meet the immediate need. He did what he could to restore the injured man by placing him on his donkey, taking him to an inn, and caring for him. The Samaritan paid the innkeeper two full days' wages to care for him. He then promised to return, so he could know the man was well and cover any additional expenses. Jesus chose those actions to serve as an example for us.

Today some believe the legal system is not a place for Christians to be involved. *Let the government address these needs. The church should avoid the state.* But the legal needs of the poor—along with their spiritual needs—are not just an issue for state action. This is an issue of justice, and the church should lead the way.

As Franklin Graham says, "I believe the focus on providing for human needs has diminished the message we are supposed to carry as good Samaritans. . . . Our purpose in responding to crises around the world is not to help the government provide housing and soup kitchens for refugees, our purpose is to work with people through the storms that beset them to earn the right to proclaim the love of Jesus Christ. This is what compels us to meet the needs of others and to do it unashamedly."[6]

Along life's Jericho Road we have unexpected opportunity to serve broken, hurting people. A sinful world has left them trapped by circumstances and choices that immobilize them. They watch helplessly as others pass them by, and they wonder if anyone cares. And they are in our neighborhood. Will you use what you have to serve the injured? Will you choose to be a Samaritan?

Hundreds of volunteers join our organization every year. They bake cookies for clients, fold pamphlets, provide interpretation, answer phones, enter data, draft letters, clean, assist with technology, help with communications. They greet clients and help them with forms. They pray for clients, staff, and volunteers. They become financial counselors, mediators, or tax advisers. They are students, moms, retired people, and others who wish to use their gifts to serve the wounded. Every role is important.

George answered our office phone. The caller, Henry, was scared and needed help. He began asking George a series of questions.

"Sir, I'm a retired electrician," George said. "You don't want me giving you any legal advice, but let me get some information and make an appointment so you can talk to one of our attorneys who can help you."

While getting Henry's information, George raised his spirits through appropriate laughter. George's laughter is contagious. Laughter is a wonderful remedy for fear.

George was a good man, a good provider, and a hard worker. After he retired, his granddaughter persuaded him to take her to church. The church in his retirement community invited me to speak. I talked about justice for the poor, how we each can make a difference, and asked for volunteers. George agreed.

Three months later, George accepted Christ, and six months later he was baptized. Several years later, George continues to make reminder calls to our clients and to encourage them in the midst of their trials.

A week after speaking with George, Henry came to the office. Liz greeted him with a warm smile, handed him papers, and offered him coffee and cookies. Henry sat on the sofa and began to relax as he looked around him.

The door into the offices opened, and a middle-aged woman smiled at him. "Hi Henry, my name is Judith, and I'm an attorney. Please follow me and we will see how we can help you."

He noticed the large painting of a soaring eagle with the words, "Those who *hope* in the Lord will renew their strength. They will soar on wings like eagles" (Isaiah 40:31, italics added). As Judith led him to an office, they passed people busy with others, but all smiled at him.

Judith entered an office looking out over beautiful trees. They sat at a round table, and Henry felt comfortable telling his story.

Depressed and broken, Henry had made poor choices financially. He had retired early from an airline, only to have them go bankrupt, resulting in the loss of 75 percent of his pension. Henry had spent his severance on a variety of business ventures that all failed. Mounting depression fueled increased medical bills. Henry's wife, Susan, was disabled, and he could not provide for them. Now the IRS was pursuing them for failure to file taxes. What could he do? At age 60, how could he obtain regular employment? He felt broken, bleeding, and alone.

Judith, the attorney, was a young widow. She had returned to law school as a second career. While she was in school, her husband was diagnosed with brain cancer. As a young mother, what could she do? As her husband was dying, she received significant support from her church and others, so she knew how important it was to be present in the midst of suffering. She wanted to use her legal skills to serve others.

Judith encountered Administer Justice when a judge had suggested she consider volunteering with us. Amazed by the opportunity to use her growing legal skills, she began volunteering regularly. After graduation she continued volunteering for a couple of years, then joined the staff. Judith could have chosen to walk past the injured. She chose to stop.

After his meeting with her, Henry wrote, "I came to Judith an emotional mess, not knowing where to go, but left with lots of information and feeling like there was hope. With Judith and God's help, things are really looking up."

Judith intervened concerning the professional need that brought Henry to the point of desperation—notices from the IRS—but she realized he needed more. She soothed the immediate wounds, but also made certain he and his wife were served beyond that need by plugging them into a church where they could receive ongoing help. She connected them with social service providers who could assist with practical needs, the Veterans Administration for help with hearing aids, an accountant for no-cost help in preparing taxes, and our financial counselors for empowerment going forward.

WE ARE ALL SAMARITANS IN NEED OF SAMARITANS

Sometimes those injured are our volunteers—an important reminder that none of us is immune from life's challenges. I met Laura at the chiropractor's office where she worked. As I waited, I would share how our work touched the lives of people trapped in injustice. Laura was taken by what we did, and began volunteering one day a week helping with data entry and client correspondence. One day Laura entered my office and asked if we could talk. She was preparing to leave her husband. She could no longer put up with his anger. She had written a letter that she intended to leave behind for him and wanted my opinion.

I asked if she believed that with God all things are possible. She did. Then I asked that she not leave, but instead talk to her husband about our mediation program. We prayed, and she agreed. She tore up the letter and got excited because she believed "God's finally going to fix Ray."

I contacted two of our volunteer mediators, Brent and Linda, to see if they would meet Ray and Laura.

Brent is a busy attorney, but he has a great heart for peace-making. Linda was a busy accountant, but she also agreed to complete our male and female mediation team. They began meeting regularly as Laura continued to push on Ray's anger issues and lack of church involvement.

Brent and Linda challenged each of them. They would talk and pray together, before and after sessions, that God would reveal Himself. Often what mediators plan is superseded by the plans of the Holy Spirit. As Laura says:

Then came the day—July 31, 2004—that God turned my world upside-down. That was the day He removed the scales from my eyes, gave me spiritual ears to hear, and pierced my hardened heart. The mediators reminded us that Jesus was present in the room, pointing to an empty chair as they always did, and then brought me to two Scriptures.

The first was John 14:15, "If you love me, you will obey what I command." At that moment the floodgates opened and I began to weep.

The second Scripture was Isaiah 6:5, "Woe to me! . . . I am ruined! For I am a man of unclean lips, and I live among a people of unclean lips, and my eyes have seen the King, the Lord Almighty."

At that moment, I was experiencing Hebrews 4:12, "For the word of God is living and active. Sharper than any double-edged sword, it penetrates even to dividing soul and spirit, joints and marrow; it judges the thoughts and attitudes of the heart."

With crystal clarity I became acutely aware of my flagrant disobedience to God's word, how selfish and self-absorbed I had become.

I was overcome with a deep and profound sense of grief: first for wounding my Savior, second for wounding Ray. God was able to come in and begin the healing process.

It wasn't Ray the Lord needed to fix. It was me. The year following we experienced the best year of our marriage ever. God revealed truths I had never considered, like what an awesome provider Ray was, how generous he is to me and others, how trustworthy and responsible. I began to fall in love with him all over again. With a godly perspective, I learned to appreciate the man Ray is. I learned that miracles happen, restoration occurs, and, most importantly, God is glorified.

Two years later I asked Laura to go through mediation training. With a male volunteer mediator, she was able to help another couple reconcile and restore their relationship. We are all wounded travelers, in need of Samaritans who will stop and make a difference.

WE ALL WANT TO MAKE A DIFFERENCE

Pastor and writer Max Lucado says, "Down deep all of us want to make a difference. It's not enough just to do well, we really want to do good."[7]

The people who volunteer with Administer Justice make a difference. One student volunteer was so captivated by the need for justice, he decided to immediately serve with International Justice Mission in India and now in Washington, D.C. Others have joined legal aid organizations across the country.

The Samaritan had no concern for himself or the unjust response that might come because he was a Samaritan. At great personal cost, he stopped to make a difference.

The Samaritan, perhaps a traveling merchant, could have decided he was too busy. He could have allowed his fear of the high crime area to justify hurrying past. He could have allowed the hatred between Jews and Samaritans to poison his own response. He did not. He saw a person in need.

The priest and the Levite responded out of their self-interest. The Samaritan responded out of the interest of the wounded. That is why he did not simply apply a bandage, but made certain the man was restored by transporting him to an inn and investing in his life.

Where the legal establishment failed to demonstrate justice and the church establishment failed to demonstrate love, the Samaritan showed both. He did not think of himself, but thought of serving his wounded brother.

If you have any encouragement from being united with Christ, if any comfort from his love, if any fellowship with the Spirit, if any tenderness and compassion, then make my joy complete by being like-minded, having the same love, being one in spirit and purpose. Do nothing out of selfish ambition or vain conceit, but in humility consider others better than yourselves. Each of you should look not only to your own interests, but also to the interests of others. (Philippians 2:1–4)

Serving others involves using wisely what the Lord has given us. Each of us has the same amount of time, and we will be held accountable for how we use it. Are we building bigger barns that will one day burn and disappear—or are we building into others for eternity? (See Luke 12:13–21.) We each have different gifts and abilities. Are we burying those gifts or using them for the kingdom?

LESSON THREE: HOW THE SAMARITAN SERVED

The Samaritan served without hesitation. He did whatever was needed to see an injured man restored. "As thunder follows lightning," Randy Alcorn says in *The Treasure Principle*, "giving follows grace. When God's grace touches you, you can't help but respond with generous giving."[8]

The Samaritan of Luke 17 was touched by God's healing grace, and he gave thanks. A thankful heart is a giving heart. We give because He gave. As we recognize His grace in our lives, we respond with glad, generous giving.

God's grace has filled me with peace and joy. I am often asked how I could give so much. In the world's view, I have given up hundreds of thousands of dollars, but what have I lost? I still have food, shelter, and clothes. There is nothing I want that money can buy.

What I want is a sense of purpose. I want to know that what I am doing matters to God and serves others. I want a wife who loves, respects, and serves alongside me. I want children who know God and live that out daily. Money can't buy that, and if I'm not careful it can create problems in each of those areas.

Too often we fall into the trap of measuring ourselves by our monetary worth.

WHAT I WANT IS A SENSE OF PURPOSE. I WANT TO KNOW THAT WHAT I AM DOING MATTERS TO GOD AND SERVES OTHERS.

When my sons were eight, they were talking with a friend while my wife drove them to an event. "What does your dad do?" the boy asked.

"Our dad's a lawyer," Joseph said.

The boy's eyes grew big. "You guys must be rich."

"Nah," Daniel said. "Our daddy's a free lawyer. He helps people."

"That stinks."

A free lawyer doesn't make sense to an eight-year-old, but it means a great deal to an eighty-year-old.

Mary was overwrought. The calls about her bills were constant, and she could not sleep. She received an official looking notice from a company saying she would be sentenced to prison if she did not pay. A widow for many years, Mary lived alone in a subsidized apartment. Her only income was a small Social Security check. What could she do? Her priest referred her to us.

Mary met with a financial counselor, who thought the notice seemed wrong. The counselor spoke with one of the attorneys, who contacted the creditor. With some probing, the attorney found the company had bought very old debt at pennies on the dollar and was simply going after people who had the same name.

Mary had a common last name, and it was obvious the debt was not hers. Thankful, Mary sent us a card with a note and a five-dollar bill, saying, "Please accept this donation toward your good work for the poor and unfortunate." Mary gave the widow's mite.

The widow in Luke 21 trusted God for her provision and gave all she had. The wealthy gave only out of their surplus, keeping more than they needed. The widow realized all she had came from God, so she gladly returned it to Him.

The disciples who saw this missed the point and began pointing out the beautiful stones and gifts in the temple. Jesus spoke to the heart of the matter, saying all those stones would crumble and everything on earth will disappear when He returns. He concluded, "Don't spend all of your time thinking about eating or drinking or worrying about life. If you do, the final day will suddenly catch you like a trap. That day will surprise everyone on earth. Watch out and keep praying that you can escape all that is going to happen and that the Son of Man will be pleased with you" (Luke 21:34–36 CEV).

We all need the widow's mite. Compared to the rest of the world, we have great wealth that easily entangles us. Giving is freeing. Giving means trusting God instead of ourselves. Giving means living as if today may be the day the Lord returns. On that day, what will a large home, nice cars, big screen TVs, or other stuff get us? There is an eternal reward for those who give generously to advancing the kingdom.

"Good will come to him who is generous and lends freely, who conducts his affairs with justice" (Psalm 112:5). The Samaritan was generous with his time and treasure. He conducted his affairs with justice. He is a model for us all.

THE SAMARITAN'S CHALLENGE

I have learned much from the Samaritan. Possibly a traveling businessman, he was taking a risk in traveling through an area where he would not be well received. That did not stop the Samaritan. But God did.

The Samaritan was in the middle of carrying out his plans. But seeing an injured neighbor, he took time away from that plan to serve. Legal assistance for the poor began in this country because businessmen saw a need and stopped to do something about it. Today Administer Justice benefits from businesspeople who are creative, innovative, and generous. They serve in advisory functions to help with strategic growth. They provide generous financial support. They involve their employees and others. They make a difference with their time, influence, and resources.

Like these business leaders, the Samaritan took a risk. He didn't wait to calculate its extent, but immediately decided on a course of action. That course included not only immediate aid, but ongoing support as he spent the rest of the day and night caring for the man. He provided two days' wages and promised more if needed. He made certain the man was in good hands before he resumed his venture.

Will you take the Samaritan challenge? Will you take a risk to serve the injured? You could begin with providing two days' wages to the work of justice for the poor. Many can do much more.

My new friend, Joe, was recently named entrepreneur of the year for his innovative team-building business strategies. Joe is not ashamed of the gospel and built his business on that foundation.

Joe involves his whole family in the ministry of giving. As a family, they believe God has called them to live out Matthew 25, which includes the parable of the talents and the parable of the sheep and goats. They ask themselves if they are investing for the kingdom and serving the least of these. For his family, that means a plan to double the talents given to them so they can share these resources in the local community. Together the family prays about opportunities to make a difference in the lives of disadvantaged people with the hope of the gospel.

Jesus' final command to His disciples was: "You will be my witnesses in Jerusalem, and in all Judea and Samaria, and to the ends of the earth" (Acts 1:8). Samaria was next to Judea, but I believe Jesus was telling us to go into our backyards and serve people we might not choose to serve.

Samaria was a place Jews avoided. Rather than travel through it, they took the time to walk around it. By choosing not to bypass Samaria, by serving the least of these, Christians make a statement to a skeptical world. While the world may challenge what we say, it is difficult to challenge the fact of our actions.

It really is more blessed to give than to receive. Can you imagine a life without giving? That life would be devoid of joy. We would call such a person a scrooge, after Charles Dickens's character, Ebenezer Scrooge.

What are we working for? What legacy are we creating? The secret to joyful living is found in glad, generous giving. Scrooge learned that secret well. At the end of *A Christmas Carol*, Dickens writes:

> He became as good a friend, as good a master, and as good a man, as the good old city knew, or any other good old city, town, or borough, in the good old world. Some people laughed to see the alteration in him, but he let them laugh, and little heeded them; for he was wise enough to know that nothing ever happened on this globe, for good, at which some people did not have their fill of laughter in the outset; and knowing that such as these would be blind anyway, he thought it quite as well that they should wrinkle up their eyes in grins, as have the malady in less attractive forms. His own heart laughed: and that was quite enough for him.[9]

Some may laugh at businessmen and women who generously give hard-earned money away. Let them. You can't take money with you into eternity, but you can make a profound difference by paying it forward and investing in the kingdom.

Jesus said, "I have told you this so that my joy may be in you and that your joy may be complete. My command is this: Love each other as I have loved you. Greater love has no one than this, that he lay down his life for his friends. You are my friends if you do what I command" (John 15:11–14).

Are we doing what He commands? Are we experiencing His joy? A joy that comes from a living faith, expressed through a giving love? Will you dare to set aside your life—your agenda—to be a Samaritan?

CHAPTER 7

LESSONS FROM THE JERICHO ROAD

"A man from Samaria then came traveling along that road."
—Luke 10:33 (CEV)

"On the one hand, we are called to play the Good
Samaritan on life's roadside, but that will be only an initial
act. One day we must come to see that the whole Jericho
Road must be transformed so that men and women will
not be constantly beaten and robbed as they make their
journey on life's highway." —Martin Luther King Jr.

DEATH ROBBED HER of her husband, but fate would
not rob her of what she was owed. Undaunted by the legal system, she refused to despair. She pleaded with the judge, "Grant me
justice against my adversary." Though the judge was unconcerned
with her plight, he tired of her persistence and granted her justice.

The story, told by Jesus in Luke 18, is one we often hear at
Administer Justice. Whether they are battling an insurance company, banks, creditors, the government, or multiple other scenarios,
widows come seeking justice. The point of Jesus' story in Luke
18:1–8 is to show his disciples "they should always pray and not
give up" (Luke 18:1).

Jesus chose one of the most difficult challenges anyone can
face in our broken world—our justice system. Whether in an-
cient Palestine or contemporary America, legal systems are run
by flawed individuals. For the person crying out for justice, delay

after delay can be overwhelming. "Grant me justice against my adversary," is the cry of the broken.

Jesus knew the disciples would understand the challenges faced by a widow in the court system. They would feel her burden as time and again she returned to the judge crying out for justice.

Jesus chose an unjust worldly judge as a contrast to the perfect holy judge. "And will not God bring about justice for his chosen ones, who cry out to him day and night? Will he keep putting them off? I tell you, he will see that they get justice, and quickly" (Luke 18:7–8).

God is a god of justice.[1] Justice is part of His character.[2] Justice is the foundation of His throne.[3] Crying out to an unjust judge for justice can yield results, but crying out to the perfect judge always gets results. "He is the Rock, his works are perfect, and all his ways are just. A faithful God who does no wrong, upright and just is he" (Deuteronomy 32:4).

In our American justice system, a request of the court is called a "prayer for relief." That is the picture Jesus gives of the widow. By faith, she persistently prayed for relief.

Prayer entails an act of persistent faith as we petition the High King of heaven for justice. James makes it clear that "when you ask, you do not receive, because you ask with wrong motives" (James 4:3). While Jesus does not give details of the widow's plight, we can infer that her cause was just.

If we are to combat injustice, we must begin with persistent prayer. And that prayer must begin with examining our motives. If we are seeking to create publicity, earn recognition, or place our needs ahead of those we serve, we will fail. But if we genuinely desire to free people from the chains of injustice and provide them with a lasting hope, then that faith can and will move mountains.

Consider the story from Scripture of another widow who was

anxious because a creditor was coming to take all she had. In desperation she sought help.

The man told her to go to her neighbors and ask them to get involved. Specifically, she was to ask them for empty jars. By faith the woman went to her neighbors. House by house, she persisted in asking for help. Her sons helped her pour into the jars the last of their oil, which miraculously multiplied until all were filled. The man of God then told her to sell the oil, pay her debts, and use the remainder to live on (2 Kings 4:1–7).

Her provision matched her faith. To the extent she sought help from her neighbors, she received the blessing of provision.

Elisha could have sent her to the synagogue for benevolence. He could have prayed for immediate provision. But the widow and her boys learned much more by taking action themselves. She was empowered to seek help from neighbors. That must have been hard, but in her desperation she was willing.

She involved a community in solving her problem. Before seeking Elisha, the woman was isolated and could see only her lack of resources. But Elisha reminded her she was part of a community and could seek its assistance. Now others could join in the blessing of God's provision.

Often justice needs to be community justice,

> TO THE EXTENT SHE SOUGHT HELP FROM HER NEIGHBORS, SHE RECEIVED THE BLESSING OF PROVISION.

especially when the issues are systemic. The first level of community involvement is persistent prayer. The second is provision—using what we have, even when it's just empty jars, to make a difference.

Cornelius was a centurion in the Italian Regiment who "gave

generously to those in need and prayed to God regularly" (Acts 10:2). His faith, persistent prayers, and provision were rewarded with a vision of an angel who told him, "Your prayers and gifts to the poor have come up as a memorial offering before God" (Acts 10:4).

As a result, God would use Cornelius to end the greatest injustice in the early church—the belief that salvation belonged only to the Jews or circumcised Gentiles. When Peter saw the faith of Cornelius he responded, "I now realize how true it is that God does not show favoritism but accepts men from every nation who fear him and do what is right" (Acts 10:34–35).

Today it is difficult to understand the magnitude of Cornelius's vision and Peter's response. But the New Testament is filled with this struggle, which divided the early church. It was a source of conflict between Peter and Paul. It was why Paul was pursued, beaten, and stoned by those who believed salvation belonged only to the Jews. The division between Jews and Gentiles was the great divide of the first-century church.

In America that great divide is race, and it remains a leading contributor to injustice. In their book *Divided by Faith*, Michael Emerson and Christian Smith examine the role of white evangelicalism in race relations.[4] Based on extensive interviews and study, they conclude that the evangelical church, with its focus on individual salvation, not only misses the opportunity to break down the great divide between races, but also contributes to it.

This view is shared by my friend Ed Gilbreath, who wrote *Reconciliation Blues*. "A sad tendency of evangelical faith is to elevate the act of evangelism over the humanity of the people we want to reach . . . Apparently, any time an ethnic minority speaks out against a race-related injustice, he risks being branded a malcontent in need of therapy."[5]

Racial injustice is real. Whether the African-American is branded a criminal, the Middle Eastern man is branded a terrorist, or the Hispanic man is branded an illegal, we make judgments. And in doing so, we avoid even traveling the Jericho Road.

We must not walk on by as if racial injustice does not exist. We should listen to our neighbors of color who understand well the injustices in their community. And our friends of race should not give up, but seek opportunity to lead by example in fighting injustice.

Cornelius did. He earnestly prayed for justice, and he invested himself by helping meet material needs. Many Jews provided support out of obligation, but this Gentile did so because it was the right thing. He was a man of character, and his prayers and gifts to the poor were rewarded by the High King of heaven.

While the divide between Jew and Gentile would remain a source of contention, one man's just character, demonstrated through faithful prayers and provision, paved the way for reconciliation.

Many Christians quote Paul about how Christ "has destroyed the barrier, the dividing wall of hostility . . . to reconcile both of them to God through the cross, by which he put to death their hostility" (Ephesians 2:14, 16). Paul was writing of the divide between Jew and Gentile, but much the same division exists today across racial and social lines.

The Jericho Road is real. We must not ignore the structures that contribute toward injustice. Yet we must not forget that these barriers are destroyed through the cross. We need men and women willing to demonstrate, by word and deed, that injustice will not be accepted. Dr. Martin Luther King Jr. used the Jericho Road as a metaphor in his famous mountaintop speech where he declared, "One day we must come to see that the whole Jericho Road must be transformed so that men and women will not be constantly beaten and robbed as they make their journey on life's highway. True compassion is more than flinging a coin to a beggar. It comes to see that an edifice which produces beggars needs restructuring."

Charity is good, but justice seeks more. Justice seeks to educate, empower, and root out structures that contribute toward
injustice.

But before we battle injustice, we must first prepare ourselves.
As a centurion, Cornelius
would never have entered a battle

BUT BEFORE WE
BATTLE INJUSTICE,
WE MUST FIRST
PREPARE OURSELVES.

unprepared. In the war against
injustice we battle not with flesh
and blood, but against the powers
of this dark world and the spiritual forces of evil in the heavenly
realms (Ephesians 6:12). So we
must be strong in the Lord and in His mighty power.

> Put on the full armor of God, so that when the day of
> evil comes, you may be able to stand your ground, and
> after you have done everything, to stand. Stand firm then,
> with the belt of truth buckled around your waist, with the
> breastplate of righteousness in place, and with your feet
> fitted with the readiness that comes from the gospel of
> peace. In addition to all of this, take up the shield of faith,
> with which you can extinguish all the flaming arrows of
> the evil one. Take the helmet of salvation and the sword
> of the Spirit, which is the word of God. And pray in the
> Spirit on all occasions with all kinds of prayers and re-
> quests. With this in mind, be alert and always keep on
> praying for all the saints. (Ephesians 6:13–18)

It is no accident that Paul surrounds the famous battle metaphor in prayer. We must be alert. We must be watchful and informed. We must keep on praying.

The agents of injustice are legion. But greater is He who is in us than he who is in the world. (See 1 John 4:4.) Our great challenge is to guard our hearts in prayer that we battle for the right—and not for a holy war of our own making. As Abraham Lincoln said, "I know that the Lord is always on the side of the right. But it is my constant anxiety and prayer that I and this nation should be on the Lord's side."

This is why Paul's armor is vital. The belt of truth, the breastplate of righteousness or justice, feet fitted with the gospel of peace, the shield of faith, the helmet of salvation, and the sword of God's Word. Armed this way we can extinguish the flaming arrows of injustice. This armor allows us to stand without fear, knowing the war is already won.

This confidence has turned many a battle against injustice. Whether William Wilberforce in his fight against the English slave trade, Abraham Lincoln in his fight against slavery in America, or Martin Luther King Jr. in his fight for civil rights, all were strong men of faith who armed themselves in prayer, provided all they had, and courageously stood against injustice.

These men exemplify a humble strength of character and devotion to a just cause. Each withstood great assaults upon themselves and the cause of justice, but each prevailed because: "He will make your righteousness shine like the dawn, the justice of your cause like the noonday sun" (Psalm 37:6).

The magnitude of the subject of injustice is great. If we are to rise to Dr. King's challenge of changing the Jericho Road, we must persistently pray, provide, prepare, and pursue the battle. Then we march forward with a firm step in full assurance that God's cause will bear us out.

SEVENTEEN MILES

The Jericho Road was a steep, winding path climbing nearly 3,000 feet over the seventeen miles connecting Jericho to Jerusalem.

In the time of Jesus, the road was notorious for its danger and difficulty, and was known as the "Way of Blood" because "of the blood which is often shed there by robbers."[6]

Today the Jericho Road takes many forms.

- ▶ It is the seventeen-hour day worked by Juan and his immigrant friends as they wait to be picked up by a van in the predawn hours to work until after sunset, in hopes of supporting their family.
- ▶ It is the seventeen-year-old pregnant girl who has run away from home, and whose baby and life are in danger of abuse on the streets.
- ▶ It is the seventeen-month-old child whose father is in prison and whose mother is on drugs and needs a stable home.
- ▶ It is the seventeen-floor tenement building filled with single parents struggling to make ends meet.
- ▶ It is the seventeen blocks encompassing a minority neighborhood torn apart by gangs and violence.
- ▶ It is the seventeen grueling minutes that a mother endures before a judge, not comprehending the lifelong impact the judge's decision will have upon her child.
- ▶ It is the seventeen of forty homes in foreclosure as families live in fear of homelessness.
- ▶ It is the seventeen rooms in a nursing home under investigation for exploitation and elder abuse.
- ▶ It is the seventeen calls a day, threatening to jail a senior citizen if a debt is not paid.
- ▶ It is seventeen miles of violence, oppression, and suffering.

Addressing these injustices requires prayer, provision, preparation, planning, and perseverance. Do you remember Mary, the widow from the last chapter who sought justice from a creditor who called continuously, threatening her for a debt that proved not to be hers? These creditors, collection agencies pursuing vulnerable individuals who share the same name as another person, have come to be called zombie debt collectors. In 2007, this industry collected $110 billion.[7]

Freeing Mary from the unjust debt was critical, but it was equally important for us to help others in similar circumstances who did not know free legal assistance was available. We sought involvement of the attorney general and involved an outside attorney who handles class action lawsuits to stamp out such injustice. The company that was hounding Mary was closed down, and thousands like her were saved from being pursued for debt that was not theirs.

Financial exploitation is a common area where involving a community is necessary to combat fraud and injustice, such as the people suffering from fear in the seventeen rooms in a nursing home. Sometimes this requires tightening laws for better oversight of elder care facilities. Administer Justice involves legislators in these issues and seeks their assistance.

In most instances the challenge with our court system is not the system, but meaningful access to it. Without an advocate, many rights are lost.

When Juan came to us complaining of not being paid after working seventeen-hour days, we realized none of his friends were paid either. We arranged a meeting with the state's attorney, resulting in a special unit to investigate and prosecute this fraud. Juan was too afraid to speak with authorities, and they may not have listened, but with an advocate, several injustices were righted.

When seventeen of forty homes in one area were in foreclosure, we approached the chief judge to pull together a community group to address the problem. This resulted in a change in the court system, requiring lenders and homeowners to sit down in mediation and do everything possible to avoid another empty, ravaged home. Because they now had a voice, families were not demoralized and tempted to destroy the home. Banks were required to address in a timely manner the available options, thus reducing red tape and costs and often resulting in some agreement.

When we examined the struggles of single moms in a seventeen-floor tenement building, it became apparent that the lack of involvement by fathers was a root cause. Administer Justice approached the chief judge of the family court and together established a community committee that included area churches.

The result was a fathers' court, where delinquent dads could avoid jail for failure to pay support if they successfully completed an alternative fatherhood program. The program emphasized the importance of fatherhood, the positive influence dads have on their children, and the importance of paying support. It included pointed discussions, role playing, letter writing, and practical skills for finding and keeping a job. The result was a significant increase in the collection of support and involvement by fathers.

Within the court system, we have sought to increase access for unrepresented individuals. Now the county has built rooms in the courthouse that could be staffed by volunteer attorneys to answer legal questions, prepare forms, and coach individuals in presenting them. We encouraged the court to advocate for *pro bono* involvement by attorneys, which resulted in the court color-coding all *pro bono* files so judges could have these attorneys go first—acknowledging the important role that volunteer attorney was providing, and encouraging more involvement.

Administer Justice worked with area churches, counselors, and the court to create a resource for family counseling and divorce recovery. This was then distributed at the courthouse to encourage people to seek assistance and to involve churches in the process.

We were brought in to meet with city officials to discuss how the community could better address the problem of homes violating the zoning code. Code enforcement officials had been serving suits to elderly residents—with stiff daily penalties for continued non-compliance. Together we created an alternative, and now the officials provide a flier listing local churches that will come and do repairs and Administer Justice to aid in any legal issues.

Most challenges affect a local community, so they can be resolved by involving the community. Some challenges require changes in law on a state level and some on a federal level. The seventeen-month old child in need of guardianship and a stable home represents one state example.

Many parents who reach the point of recognizing they can't adequately care for a child lack the resources to hire an attorney and create a formal guardianship. So several legal aid groups worked together with the state legislature to define a short-term guardianship that did not require going to court. Now children can be placed voluntarily in stable homes to allow parents the opportunity to resolve issues that threaten their child's welfare. The guardianship is valid for one year but can be renewed for as long as needed.

To address the issue of court access statewide, we joined with many other legal aid groups, private bar associations, and judicial groups to change and clarify laws to allow for limited representation. Normally once an attorney is involved in a case, that attorney must remain on that case and be involved with all issues—or go through a process of withdrawing. The new rules allow an attorney to appear for a single issue—such as child support—without having to address all the issues of a case. This encourages more attorneys to provide *pro bono* assistance.

Some issues require change on a federal level. We joined others who work with low-income taxpayers in addressing issues with the government through SAMS—the Systemic Advocacy Management System. This system enables those on the front line to notify the taxpayer advocate of a recurring problem. This has led to new licensing standards for preparers, changes in notices sent by the IRS, and many other responses.

We recently assisted Paul, who had a tax liability from 1980 in the original amount of $600. Because he did not have an attorney, he was persuaded to execute a document waiving the statute of limitations for collections. He retired last year and began receiving Social Security, which the IRS garnished. He was told he now owed $53,000. Confused and overwhelmed, he found our clinic and we were able to stop the garnishing.

When we raised the issue, we learned the IRS had been directed not to continue collecting beyond the statute of limitations. We filed in tax court to relieve Paul of further liability and even achieved a refund.

> EVERY SOCIAL ISSUE—FROM MARRIAGE TO ABORTION, RELIGIOUS FREEDOM TO IMMIGRATION—INVOLVES THE LAW.

Every social issue—from marriage to abortion, religious freedom to immigration—involves the law. Those areas that affect the widow, the fatherless, the alien, and the poor are where we seek to be a voice. We filed a friend of the court brief before the United States Supreme Court on behalf of a poor mother advocating for life. We work alongside World Relief in assisting refugees. We also join in the effort to educate and advocate for comprehensive reform.

The alien within our borders suffers many injustices. Administer Justice is often criticized for assisting undocumented individuals.

Many Christians view our involvement as a failure to obey the authorities. It is not. But understanding what the authorities say is both complex and contradictory.

On one hand, our law provides that a person who entered the country without a proper status, or remained in this country and lost that status, is here unlawfully. On the other hand, Congress chose in 1984 to broaden the definition of "resident alien" for tax purposes to include anyone with a "substantial presence" within the United States.[8] That expansion recognized our lack of border patrol and sought a way to collect taxes from undocumented workers.

In 1996 the IRS created the Individual Taxpayer Identification Number (ITIN) knowing that many of the 7.3 million ITINs issued through 2004 went to unlawful residents.[9] Congress created a system for collecting taxes from undocumented workers, while not permitting them lawful work. As a result many workers use false Social Security numbers, which contributes to problems of identity theft, fraud, and abuse.

This goes both ways. Many workers are not paid for work performed, and many employers fail to report and pay taxes for work done off the books. When taxes are paid by these workers, it creates a mismatch with Social Security, so the funds are deposited in an earnings suspense file, which added $56 billion in 2002[10] to the $420 billion already in the file.[11] These funds help sustain our current system while the workers are unable to claim any of the benefits.

Low-income taxpayer clinics like ours seek to navigate this complexity by educating about the unlawful use of Social Security numbers and the need to complete taxes with ITINs. But the problems remain and grow larger every year.

The United States encourages the filing of taxes by resident aliens, but disqualifies them from the largest government benefit designed to help low-income workers—the earned income tax credit. Our government adopts laws prohibiting discrimination in education and health care, allows enforcement of alien rights in civil courts, but denies most public benefits, including public housing. So more than one family will often reside in a home.

While the burden of resident aliens is greater on local communities, these communities benefit from sales of goods and services, sales taxes, property taxes, and labor that could not be replaced were we suddenly to remove all undocumented workers from the economy.

Our office obeys the authorities. Where benefits are permitted we enforce those benefits, and where they are denied we pursue legitimate alternatives. But the system is broken. There are no lines to tell immigrants to stand in so they can become citizens. There are no simple solutions. We need to pray, study, talk to those affected, and work toward some comprehensive solution.

There are several excellent books to begin this process, including *Welcoming the Stranger: Justice, Compassion and Truth in the Immigration Debate*[12] and *Christians at the Border: Immigration, the Church and the Bible.*[13] As we get to know the alien among us, the complexities of the issue will become more apparent. Navigating those complexities is beyond the scope of this book, but meeting those affected may demonstrate some of the challenges.

Juanita learned of Administer Justice through a shelter where she was staying. She could not stop the tears as she relayed in broken English her tragic story. Months before, she was living the American dream. Scott was a young businessman who met Juanita in Brazil and fell in love. Juanita had a son, and Scott wanted them to live with him in the United States.

Juanita came to the States on a fiancé visa. She and her son moved in with Scott and his family. Before her papers could process, Scott was killed in an automobile accident. Juanita's grief was compounded when Scott's family took her son and threw all her possessions on the lawn.

Scott's family practiced voodoo. A priestess informed them the son was to replace Scott, but the mother must not be allowed to stay. Juanita was terrified. She'd learned in her country to fear the police, and she despaired of ever again seeing her son.

I spoke with Juanita about another widow who had to face her fear. She found herself in a foreign country with no resources. But she did not despair. She realized the gods of her people were not real, but believed in one God who had the power to sustain her. That faith allowed Ruth to face her fear. God saw the faith of this alien and provided a kinsman-redeemer for her. She was blessed with a great-grandson named David who would be king—and she would be part of the line of Jesus who would come to redeem not just one woman of faith, but all people.

Juanita's background was also voodoo, which is built on fear. She did not want to continue as a slave to this fear, and as we talked her spirit quickened. She wanted a faith built on love. She prayed to accept Christ. We called the police, who intervened and returned Juanita's son to her.

Peter understands Juanita's fear. His parents entered the United States on a visa from Eastern Europe when he was one year old. They overstayed this visa, leaving Peter without lawful status. All he knew was America. He had no choice in his parents' decision.

I met Peter as he was serving my sons in the youth group of our church. He pulled me aside and shared his fear. He wanted to go to college, but there was no way for him to do so since he could not obtain loans or prove citizenship. The only encouragement I could give Peter was to pray for adoption of the Development, Relief and Education for Alien Minors (DREAM) Act,[14] which would create a path to citizenship for these hard-working men and women who want to become productive citizens through a college education or military service.

While the fight over the DREAM Act continues on a federal

level, we joined many other groups in passing a state DREAM Act to provide hope to Peter and others like him. Peter can now attend college in Illinois while he prays for a path to citizenship.

Jenny understands the fear and challenges faced by Peter and Juanita. She is on staff at a large, vibrant church where no one knows of her undocumented status. Jenny discovered in her forties that she was not a US citizen. She grew up in Michigan living with her German mother and her American father, but learned her father was adoptive and not biological. He never went through the process to make Jenny a citizen.

Although current law says an adopted child of a citizen is also a citizen, the laws were different when Jenny moved to the United States as a toddler. With no ability to prove lawful entry, she faces significant challenges. Fortunately, with a professional advocate, there is hope for Jenny.

The challenges confronting the widow, the fatherless, the alien, and the poor are complex. Many of the issues arouse strong feelings. While our government system is not perfect, justice is possible without bloodshed. That is not true of many other nations.

We have a duty to "speak up for those who cannot speak for themselves, for the rights of all who are destitute" (Proverbs 31:8). As citizens of heaven we are to pray, "your kingdom come, your will be done on earth as it is in heaven" (Matthew 6:10). That kingdom will be marked by justice. That kingdom's policy on race and immigration will not create divisions based on appearance, language, or culture. Every tribe and every nation will be found in the perfect kingdom to come.

We are called to work toward that kingdom. We are called to administer justice, to show mercy and compassion. How we do that is not easy, but we must begin with a foundation of prayer. We must make provision, prepare, and pursue truth, education, and community involvement.

May our advocacy be rooted in truth and justice. May we seek the Lord fully, and may we have the courage to stand for those who cannot stand for themselves as they travel the Jericho Road. Together may we do justice, love mercy, and walk humbly with our God.

Please join me in this prayer:

O Lord of all creation, we recognize that righteousness and justice are the foundation of Your throne; that love and faithfulness go before You. Rise up, O judge of the earth; rise up and deliver the needy who cry out, the afflicted who have no one to help. Loose the chains of injustice wherever they may be found. This day we pray for our brothers and sisters around the world who are enslaved, forced to do the will of their oppressor. May they know that You hear their cries. Rescue the weak and needy; deliver them from the hands of the wicked. For we know You work righteousness and justice for all the oppressed.

O God, we pray for those who groan this day from the effects of a fallen nature, from oil spills to earthquakes, volcanoes to floods. Hear their cries. For we know that You secure justice for the poor and uphold the cause of the needy. Heal our land that justice may once again roll on like a river and righteousness as a never-ending stream.

Rise up, O judge of the earth, defend the cause of the weak and fatherless; maintain the rights of the poor and oppressed. Raise up people of faith who will do justice, love mercy, and walk humbly before You. Establish justice in our nation and in our neighborhoods. Forgive us, O Lord, when we fall short of our pledge to be one nation, under God, indivisible, with liberty and justice for all.

As we become more divided by the way we look, may we know that You judge us for how we live. Grant us peace and free us from fear. As Lady Liberty raises her torch of hope in the harbor of New York city, may the tired, the poor, and the huddled masses yearning to be free continue to find our shores a refuge and a land of freedom and opportunity.

Forgive us when we fail to provide liberty and justice for all. Help us understand the needs of the poor in our own city, and on our own block as foreclosures continue, jobs are scarce, government is stretched, and laws are complex. Grant us wisdom to love our neighbor as ourselves. Empower us to provide a cup of cold water to those in need, to provide good guidance and counsel where needed, and to hold out the hope that comes from a loving, just God.

Father, may we administer true justice; may we show mercy and compassion to one another. Where there is hate, may we show love; where there is hurt, may we bring healing; and where there is injustice, may we bring justice. For we know that good will come to him who is generous and gives freely, who conducts his affairs with justice.

May we be people of justice that reflect a God of justice this day and every day until You establish Your kingdom and right all the injustices of this world.

Amen.

CHAPTER 8

LESSONS FROM THE INN

"Then he put him on his own donkey and took him
to an inn, where he took care of him. The next morning
he gave the innkeeper two silver coins and said,
'Please take care of the man.'" —Luke 10:34–35 CEV

"And she brought forth her firstborn son, and wrapped him
in swaddling clothes, and laid him in a manger; because
there was no room for them in the inn." —Luke 2:7 KJV

HER NAME WAS MARY. She was a young, pregnant
teenager who left home to follow her boyfriend. She was poor and
temporarily homeless. Her boyfriend had a tax issue to resolve, but
she was unaware he had planned to abandon her. Where could she
turn for help?

Mary could be one of thousands who have turned to Administer Justice for help. Rather, her story is a familiar one:

And it came to pass in those days, that there went out a
decree from Caesar Augustus that all the world should
be taxed. . . . And all went to be taxed, every one into his
own city. And Joseph also went up from Galilee . . . To be
taxed with Mary his espoused wife, being great with child.
(Luke 2:1, 3–5 KJV)

Joseph planned to divorce Mary quietly because he knew he
wasn't the father of this child. But an angel appeared to him and

told him the child was conceived of the Holy Spirit. He was to give Him the name Jesus, because He will save people from their sins (Matthew 1:19–21).

Where did Mary turn for help? She and Joseph went to an inn, but there was no room for them. Bethlehem was crowded with the census, so maybe the inn was filled. But maybe there was no room for *them*—poor and very pregnant, she would likely require care and the innkeeper had other guests to attend to. Either way, Jesus was entering this world. Nothing could hold back God's redemptive plan.

The question for the church today is whether we would have room for a poor, pregnant teenager—or other weary travelers along the Jericho Road.

LESSON ONE: THE INN
IS A PLACE TO GO FOR HELP

The Samaritan in Luke 10 could not care for the wounded man alone. He needed a place where the wounded would be cared for. A place where healing could begin. A place of warmth. A place of sustenance. He took him to the inn. Today that place should be the church.

No organization on earth can or should replace the church. The church is the bride of Christ. She is to serve her husband and make their home available for the wounded and weary. The church is a gathering place of sinners.

As pastor Paul Tripp writes in *Instruments in the Redeemer's Hands*:

> What is the church? A well-led successful organization or a hospital full of diseased people? Everywhere you look, you will find couples who are struggling to love, parents who are struggling to be patient, children who are at-

tracted to temptation, and friends who battle the disappointments of imperfect relationships. This is 100% of the church's membership! The church is not a theological classroom. It is a conversion, confession, repentance, reconciliation, forgiveness and sanctification center.[1]

What a wonderful place! I can come just as I am. I don't need a theology degree. I don't have to be perfect. I don't have to pretend all is right with me. I can come weak and wounded to the inn.

The Samaritan knew this. How many places in Israel could the Samaritan go where he would not be judged for who he was? Not many. But he could go to the inn. The inn provided a place where the Samaritan could serve the wounded.

Would the church today welcome the Samaritan and the injured man? They were quite a pair. One was despised. The other was wounded. Would we open our doors to a lawyer bringing a poor, wounded person to the church for help? Bill Leslie did.

Christian legal aid began in this country because LaSalle Street Church in Chicago saw wounded and weary victims of injustice—and welcomed them. Some of them were criminals, some were innocent victims. It didn't matter to Pastor Bill Leslie. He saw an opportunity to serve the injured.

The church had wonderful compassion ministries that met physical needs, but Pastor Leslie wanted to address the deeper need for justice. "I saw all those verses in the Bible about justice and the poor and I also saw the injustices around here."[2]

One of his heroes had been a pastor who believed the same. Dietrich Bonhoeffer said, "We are not to simply bandage the wounds of victims beneath the wheels of injustice, we are to drive a spoke into the wheel itself."

Leslie believed the church could make a difference in the Cabrini Green neighborhood. He also knew he needed the help of a specialist to combat personal and systemic injustice. He needed a lawyer.

Pastor Leslie raised the money, and the church and the community were changed.

Writer Philip Yancey described LaSalle Street as one of the most genuine churches he had ever attended. The homeless, the poor, and single mothers all sat alongside white suburbanites. The community came to the church because the church went into the community. As Yancey said, "I learned that the mission of the church extends to the needs of its own neighborhood."[3]

David Platt is pastor of Brook Hills Church in Birmingham, Alabama. His book *Radical* challenges Christians and the church to live with less and give more. He encourages applying the Great Commandment to love God and our neighbor through the Great Commission to go into all the world and make disciples:

> For each one of us, this clearly begins at home. Wherever you and I live, we are commanded to go and make disciples there. In light of Jesus' example, our primary impact on the nations will occur in the disciple making we do right around us . . . Therefore, our homes, communities, and cities are the primary places and contain the primary people with whom we will impact nations for the glory of Christ.[4]

BID THEM COME

The best way to attract weak and wounded people to the church is to meet them where they are and invite them. Let them know they are welcome. This is a place they can come, no matter who they are, to receive rest for their souls. There is room at the inn. Do you believe that?

There is a story told of a Mexican immigrant who was heavily burdened. He had risked his life to come to America and was working in the fields to send funds to his impoverished family.

The hours were long and he was weary. Walking down a dirt road he thought he heard music. As he continued he could make out the words.

". . . how sweet the sound, that saved a wretch like me . . . I once was lost but now am found, was blind, but now, I see."

Though he spoke little English he knew the words well, and his soul quickened. Somehow the dirt and sweat of the day mattered little as he neared the beautiful church.

"Through many dangers, toils and snares, we have already come. 'Tis grace that brought me safe thus far . . . and grace will lead me home."

He walked into the back of the church and was about to join in the singing when a deacon approached.

"Son, you can't come in here." He eyed the dark-skinned man, dirty and sweating.

"But . . ."

Before he could utter another word, a couple of other men gently grabbed his arm and led him outside as the music continued behind him.

Outside the man sat on the steps, head in his hands, and cried. He felt a hand on his shoulder and looked into the face of a dark-skinned man with tear-filled eyes.

A nail-pierced hand helped him up, and Jesus said to the man, "My son. Do not be discouraged. I have been trying to get into that church for years."

IS THE CHURCH A PLACE OF JUSTICE?

In his book *Generous Justice*, pastor Tim Keller advocates the important connection between justification and justice. The church should not be a place for *just us*, but a place of *justice*. Evangelism should go hand in hand with acts of justice and mercy.

> When a city perceives a church as existing strictly and
> only for itself and its own members, the preaching of that
> church will not resonate with outsiders. But if neighbors
> see church members loving their city through astonishing,
> sacrificial deeds of compassion, they will be much more
> open to the church's message. Deeds of mercy and jus-
> tice should be done out of love, not simply as a means to
> the end of evangelism. And yet there is no better way for
> Christians to lay a foundation for evangelism than by do-
> ing justice.[5]

Doing justice demonstrates love and destroys barriers in a community. A church that exists only to build itself up will not change a community. When the church is more interested in *just us* than justice, then its preaching will not resonate with outsiders.

Today the church has unprecedented opportunity to engage in gospel justice ministry that transforms individuals and communities. Every city, suburb, and rural area needs justice. Many suburban churches make the mistake of believing they must adopt an inner-city church to serve the poor. That is simply not true.

For the first time in history, the number of poor individuals living in the suburbs exceeds the number of poor living in inner cities.[6] Serve where God has placed you. Begin in your neighborhood.

Deb did. Her friend Joan was in her small group. Deb knew Joan's daughter, Sherry, and two granddaughters had recently moved in with her. Joan had asked for prayers through the divorce as Sherry escaped the alcoholic abuse of her husband.

The divorce process left them homeless. Sherry had MS and could not work, though she regularly volunteered in the church nursery. Outside of Joan's small group, the large suburban church was unaware of her needs.

Joan was asking for prayer for her granddaughters. Sherry desperately wanted to keep them in their school and provide them with stability and continuity with their friends. Both girls were doing well and were active in cheerleading. But a rival cheerleading mother called the school to let them know the girls were no longer living in the district.

The district set a hearing to expel the girls. The girls had been through so much, and Joan could not bear to think of their world being further torn apart.

Across the nation, homelessness is growing. The majority of the homeless live in doubled-up circumstances with friends or relatives. I live in a small suburban city of 120,000 residents that served more than 1,600 homeless children in 2010–11.[7] Every school system in the country has a homeless liaison to address these issues. Chances are, homeless people attend your church. They certainly live in your community.

There is help available. Joan's granddaughters are still in their school because a volunteer stepped in to persuade the district that the girls fell under the federal McKinney-Vento Homeless Assistance Act,[8] which creates stability for these children and provides support for the parents. The poor live among you. You can serve them wherever the Lord has placed you.

Churches in rural areas need to build community because the resources are more scarce. Churches in the city need to reproduce themselves in the city. Cities have different cultures than suburban or rural communities. God has placed you in a location for a reason. Wherever you are you will find needs within a short distance.

Among those will be the need for low-income legal assistance. Will you open the doors to a Samaritan? Will you open your doors to a wounded victim? Is there room in the inn?

LESSON TWO: THE INN IS
A PLACE FOR RESTORATION

The Samaritan needed a place to take the wounded victim. He went to the inn. Once he arrived, he needed to know the man would be restored. The Samaritan spent the remainder of that day and night caring for the wounded man.

The Samaritan paid the innkeeper two days' wages and promised more if needed. He pleaded, "Please take care of the man" (Luke 10:35 CEV). Only when he knew the man would be restored did he continue on his business, promising to return.

The church is the place where restoration occurs. Lawyers are like Samaritans. The ministry of Christian legal aid finds victims of injustice and binds their wounds. But ongoing restoration takes place in the church. The lawyer needs a place to send the wounded man.

The prophet Ezekiel pictures God's concern for restoring His people. "I will search for the lost and bring back the strays. I will bind up the injured and strengthen the weak, but the sleek and the strong I will destroy. I will shepherd the flock with justice" (Ezekiel 34:16).

If the church is the bride of Christ, why does she not shepherd the flock with justice? Pastor Keller says:

> Many believe that the job of the church is not to do justice at all, but to preach the Word, to evangelize, and build up believers. But if it is true that justice and mercy to the poor are the inevitable signs of justifying faith, it is hard to believe that the church is not to reflect this duty corporately in some way. And as soon as you get involved in the lives of people—in evangelism as well as spiritual nurture—you will come upon people with practical needs. You can't love people in word only (cf. 1 John 3:16–17)

and therefore you can't love people as you are doing evangelism and discipleship without meeting practical and material needs through deeds.[9]

When we fail to bind up the injured or go into our community to search for the lost, we lack love. As Ezekiel warned, "You have not strengthened the weak or healed the sick or bound up the injured. You have not brought back the strays or searched for the lost. You have ruled them harshly and brutally" (Ezekiel 34:4).

Sometimes the church finds itself in this position because, like the priest, we get so busy in the business of the church that we miss a divine opportunity. But sometimes the church finds itself in this position because, like the Levite, we forget we are all sinners saved by grace. This was the error of Israel's religious leaders.

The Pharisees believed they knew God's plan. They were righteous. They kept the law. But Jesus continually challenged these religious leaders.

Luke tells of when Jesus went to eat in the house of a prominent Pharisee. He was being carefully watched because it was the Sabbath. The Pharisees brought a man before Jesus who was crippled, and Jesus healed him. This angered the Pharisees, who accused Jesus of violating the law. But Jesus went right to the heart of the law.

When you give a luncheon or dinner, do not invite your friends, your brothers or relatives, or your rich neighbors; if you do, they may invite you back and so you will be repaid. But when you give a banquet, invite the poor, the crippled, the lame, the blind, and you will be blessed. Although they cannot repay you, you will be repaid at the resurrection of the righteous. (Luke 14:12–14)

Righteousness is not found in dogmatic adherence to the law, but in grace demonstrated through mercy to the poor and disadvantaged. Do we heal and restore the wounded—or do we cater to the rich?

John warned us not to love only "with words or tongue but with actions and in truth." And the actions were specific: "If anyone has material possessions and sees his brother in need but has no pity on him, how can the love of God be in him?" (1 John 3:17–18).

James also challenged the church, accusing them of insulting the poor, ignoring them, giving preference to the rich, and exercising a faith without deeds. He said a faith that did not meet the needs of the poor and destitute was dead. While they believed they were religious, James said plainly, "Religion that God our Father accepts as pure and faultless is this: to look after orphans and widows in their distress and to keep oneself from being polluted by the world" (James 1:27).

THE BIBLICAL CALL TO GOSPEL JUSTICE

From the beginning of Genesis to the end of Revelation, the Bible is about justice. Justice is part of who God is and what He does.

God's character demands justice. The Lord is a righteous judge (2 Timothy 4:8). The works of His hands are faithful and just (Psalm 111:7). He is the Rock, His works are perfect, and all His ways are just. A faithful God who does no wrong, upright and just is He (Deuteronomy 32:4). Morning by morning He dispenses His justice (Zephaniah 3:5).

Righteousness and justice are the foundation of His throne (Psalm 97:2). He will bring justice to the nations (Isaiah 42:1). For with the Lord our God there is no injustice or partiality or bribery (2 Chronicles 19:7). The Lord secures justice for the poor and upholds the cause of the needy (Psalm 140:12).

With righteousness He will judge the needy, with justice He will give decisions for the poor of the earth (Isaiah 11:4). He is the helper of the fatherless (Psalm 10:14). The Lord is a refuge for the oppressed, a stronghold in times of trouble (Psalm 9:8).

The Lord is our judge, the Lord is our lawgiver, the Lord is our king; it is He who will save us (Isaiah 33:22).

God in His justice created man. He established one law: to not eat from the Tree of the Knowledge of Good and Evil. Man violated God's law. Sin entered the world. But in justice, God is restoring all things. "For he has set a day when he will judge the world with justice by the man he has appointed. He has given proof of this to all men by raising him from the dead" (Acts 17:31).

On that day of judgment we will go to court and lose our case without an advocate. The Bible says of God, "Your words will be proven true, and in court you will win your case" (Romans 3:4 CEV).

We all break God's law and deserve punishment. He is willing to extend grace. "If we confess our sins, he is faithful and just and will forgive us" (1 John 1:9). We are forgiven through the sacrifice of Jesus. He becomes our advocate, the atoning sacrifice for our sins. (See 1 John 2:1–2.) Our Holy Judge imputes His righteousness through the sacrifice of His son to pardon our sins. This is God's justice.

But justice does not end with God's justice.

God created man in His image, so justice is to be part of our character. Justice is to be part of our conduct. And justice is to be part of our court.

Our character should reflect God's: "Blessed are they who maintain justice, who constantly do what is right" (Psalm 106:3). "The righteous care about justice for the poor, but the wicked have no such concern" (Proverbs 29:7). "Cursed is the man who withholds justice from the alien, the fatherless or the widow" (Deuteronomy 27:19).

Our conduct is to reflect God's as we act justly, love mercy, and walk humbly with our God (see Micah 6:8). We are to administer true justice and show mercy and compassion to one another (Zechariah 7:9). For evil people do not understand justice, but those who follow the Lord understand it completely (Proverbs 28:5).

We are called to reflect the character of our Creator. But justice does not end with personal justice. Our laws should reflect His.

God commands us to not deny justice to the poor in court (Exodus 23:6), pervert justice and show partiality (Deuteronomy 16:19), or malign or oppress the needy (Psalm 12:5). He established laws to prevent abuse of the widow, the fatherless, the alien, and the poor, and to provide for them through the law of gleaning, which left food for them to earn (Deuteronomy 24:17–22).

We are told over and over to defend the cause of the poor and needy (Psalm 82:3–4), speak up for the destitute (Proverbs 31:8–9), and intercede on their behalf as Christ intercedes on ours. They need an advocate just as we do. In God's justice they need Jesus. In man's justice they need a lawyer.

As God redeems us, we are called to redeem the law and work toward the justice He desires.

LIVING LIKE A FAITHFUL SPOUSE

Man was created in God's image, and woman from man. The Bible uses this imagery for the holy community that is the church. The church is made from God and for God. The people of God become one with God as part of a community of faith (Ephesians 5:32). As the bride of Christ, we become one with Him. We care about the things He cares about. We must have a concern for the poor that is demonstrated through just character, just conduct, and justice in the courts of man.

As Dr. Tony Evans advocates in his book *Oneness Embraced*,

"The role of the church, as a participant in God's socio-political kingdom and as His bride, is to execute divine justice on behalf of the defenseless, poor, and oppressed."[10]

The parable of the Good Samaritan was prompted by the Great Question—how can I inherit eternal life?—which led to the Great Command and effectively the Great Commission.

The Great Command calls us to love God with all our heart, mind, soul, and strength. This requires putting God first in all things. He is the only way to heaven. God's justice and grace restore us in mercy and righteousness. The gospel is primary.

But as we are transformed into the image of Jesus Christ, we reflect God's justice in our actions toward others. We demonstrate mercy. We stop and bind the wounded. We love our neighbor as ourselves. We reflect God's justice toward us in justice to our neighbor.

> SERVING OUR NEIGHBOR NATURALLY LEADS US TO THE GREAT COMMISSION.

Serving our neighbor naturally leads us to the Great Commission. It compels us to "go and do likewise." As we demonstrate love, mercy, compassion, and justice, we are compelled to share the hope of the gospel. We will seek to make disciples of all nations, baptizing them in the name of the Father and of the Son and of the Holy Spirit, and teaching them to obey everything He has commanded us (Matthew 28:19–20).

And what did He command us? To love God and our neighbor. And the circle begins anew.

This is gospel justice. This is a call for every church and every Christian.

LESSON 3: THE INN IS NOT OUR HOME

The church is a vital part of God's plan for justice. We need the inn. We need a place to be restored. But we do not live there. The church is not where we stop; the church is where we start. The church equips us for our journey along the Jericho Road.

Sometimes we get so caught up in the business of church that we miss the divine opportunities God has for us. Like the priest, we praise God for the great work happening in our church—and miss the opportunity to serve victims of injustice. The church becomes our house and we fail to see the needs around us. We live in a gated community.

I know the danger. I grew up in the church. My father was a pastor, and we lived next door to the church in a home owned by the church. People were always in our house, and we were always in the church.

That is not always a good thing. I remember the time my brother and I were playing with cars, rolling them along the hardwood floors under the pews. That might not have been bad if Dad hadn't been in the middle of a sermon.

If you want a lesson on the wrath of God, I can share one. We heard a booming, "Boys, this is the house of God—not your house. Stop playing!"

The church is God's house, not ours. We treat the church as our house, doing what we want and coming and going as we please. We play the music we want, host parties and events, and invite only the people we want. We make certain our house looks beautiful and go to great expense to build bigger and better houses of worship. There is nothing wrong with wealth or large, beautiful churches. The danger lies in forgetting whose house this is, and in spending money to our glory.

The disciples forgot. They marveled at how the temple was adorned with beautiful stones and with gifts dedicated to God.

But Jesus said, "As for what you see here, the time will come when not one stone will be left on another; every one of them will be thrown down" (Luke 21:6).

Like the disciples it is easy to get caught up in externals like the quality of music, the effectiveness of videos, and the quantity of programming—and forget that none of those is of lasting value.

The prophet Amos delivered God's warning about forgetting:

> I hate, I despise your religious feasts; I cannot stand your assemblies. Even though you bring me burnt offerings and grain offerings, I will not accept them. Though you bring choice fellowship offerings, I will have no regard for them. Away with the noise of your songs! I will not listen to the music of your harps. But let justice roll on like a river, righteousness like a never-failing stream! (Amos 5:21–24)

God despises our religious practices that are not rooted in justice and righteousness—reflected in loving God and loving our neighbor.

God cares nothing for programs. He does not measure success by numbers. God looks to the heart. He desires mercy, not sacrifice. He desires a heart that reflects His heart of justice for the poor and needy. He wants His bride, the church, to reflect His character. He wants the church to pour out justice and righteousness like life-giving water into the deserts of our communities.

The early church reflected God's heart for justice. As Philip Yancey says:

> How easily we forget that the Christian church was the first institution in the history of the world to bring together on equal footing Jews and Gentiles, men and women, slaves and free. The earliest Christians broke down barriers.

Unlike most other religions, Christians welcomed men and
women alike. The Greeks excluded slaves from most social
groupings, while Christians included them. The Jewish
temple separated worshipers by race and gender; Christians brought them together around the Lord's table.[11]

The Lord's table brings us together in the Lord's house. His
shed blood and broken body destroy all barriers. All who proclaim
Him as Lord can sit at that table in His house. Every tribe and
every nation is invited.

The church is not perfect. Paul knew that. The Corinthian
church treated the Lord's table as their own. They separated rich
and poor. They treated the house of God like their own. "Don't
you have homes to eat and drink in?" Paul said. "Or do you despise
the church of God and humiliate those who have nothing?" (1
Corinthians 11:22).

Let's not humiliate the poor. Instead, let them know that God
loves them so much, He sent His one and only Son to die for
them. Let's demonstrate God's love, mercy, compassion, and justice. Let's make the most of the divine opportunity to welcome a
Samaritan—and an injured man—to our inn.

LESSON 4: THE INN
EQUIPS PEOPLE FOR THE JOURNEY

The inn was a community gathering spot. Travelers would
stop there to be fed and speak to others about the events of the
day. The inn was a place of hospitality. The inn was a temporary
home away from home designed to strengthen and equip travelers
for their continuing journey.

The innkeeper judged neither the Samaritan nor his injured
companion. He welcomed them, fed them, equipped the Samaritan for his continuing travels, and cared for the injured man.

Today the church should be the place where weary travelers are refreshed, fed, and sent on their journey. The church must proclaim the Word. Travelers must be able to understand not only what is happening around them, but also how the Word of God addresses the issues of our day.

> **TODAY THE CHURCH SHOULD BE THE PLACE WHERE WEARY TRAVELERS ARE REFRESHED, FED, AND SENT ON THEIR JOURNEY.**

The church needs to feed its travelers. This includes not only proclaiming the Word, but also equipping people through discipleship. This is why community is important as we grow together in the Word and through corporate prayer and worship.

But we need to think of the church not as a destination, but as a critically important stop along the Jericho Road. The church equips us for our journey. The church arms us for the battle.

We are at war. Our enemy is always mobilizing his forces to outflank us. He wants to divide and destroy churches, Christian businesses, Christian homes, and Christian people. He turns brother against brother.

Pastor David Platt uses a wonderful analogy in his book *Radical*. The SS *United States* was designed to be the world's fastest and most reliable troop carrier. But it never served that purpose. Instead it was converted into a luxury cruise ship.

Platt writes, "When I think about the history of the SS *United States*, I wonder if she has something to teach me about the history of the church. The church, like the SS *United States*, has been designed for battle. The purpose of the church is to mobilize a people to accomplish a mission. Yet we seem to have turned the church as troop carrier into the church as luxury liner."[12]

In *Churches that Make a Difference*, theologian Ron Sider writes, "What holds you back from taking the first small step toward leading your congregation to transform your community through evangelism and social ministry? The God of the Bible wants it. Our hurting society needs it. In the power and love of the Spirit, we can do it."[13]

If we are not equipping our people to perform good works, which God prepared in advance for us to do (Ephesians 2:10), then we are in danger of having the type of church the prophet Ezekiel warned of.

> My people come to you, as they usually do, and sit before you to listen to your words, but they do not put them into practice. With their mouths they express devotion, but their hearts are greedy for unjust gain. Indeed, to them you are nothing more than one who sings love songs with a beautiful voice and plays an instrument well, for they hear your words but do not put them into practice. (Ezekiel 33:31–32)

We want generous Christians who overflow with God's grace. God's grace makes us just. In justice we serve our wounded neighbor. We equip God's people for the battle. We join the battle against injustice.

Martin Luther said, "What is it to serve God and to do His will? Nothing else than to show mercy to our neighbor. For it is our neighbor who needs our service; God in heaven needs it not."

TAKING INVENTORY

The inn could help no one if it was not properly stocked. We must always be prepared to give an answer to everyone who asks us to give the reason for the hope that we have (1 Peter 3:15). We must continuously be in the Word so we can train others. We must know why justice is important.

A group of pastors formed The Gospel Coalition to equip ministry leaders to take inventory. They help stock healthy churches. One of the required items is equipping the church for gospel service in the community by doing justice and mercy. They write:

> We cannot look at the poor and the oppressed and callously call them to pull themselves out of their own difficulty. Jesus did not treat us that way. The gospel replaces superiority toward the poor with mercy and compassion. Christian churches must work for justice and peace in their neighborhoods through service even as they call individuals to conversion and the new birth. We must work for the eternal and common good and show our neighbors we love them sacrificially whether they believe as we do or not. Indifference to the poor and disadvantaged means there has not been a true grasp of our salvation by sheer grace.[14]

USING SPECIALISTS

In addition to training our church leaders so they can equip God's people, we need to partner with specialist organizations. Pastor Max Lucado says this well:

> "Poverty," as Rich Stearns, president of World Vision in the United States, told me, "is rocket science." Simple solutions simply don't exist.... Most of us don't know what to do, but someone does! Some people are pouring every ounce of God-given wisdom into the resolution of these problems. We need specialist organizations, such as World Vision, Compassion International, Living Water, and International Justice Mission.[15]

Administer Justice is a specialist organization in the Chicago area. Gospel Justice Initiative is a national association that serves to engage the church in matters of law and justice.

Lawyers and others need tools and training to make the most of the opportunity to serve victims of injustice. The legal needs of the poor are complex, but a partnership with Gospel Justice Initiative provides the resources to provide legal help and gospel hope.

At the same time as the church shows mercy to the needy, the Samaritan can serve the church. While the innkeeper provided life-saving assistance to the wounded man, the Samaritan provided something of value to him. Sometimes the church needs the help that a Samaritan can provide.

As an attorney, my area of expertise was church law, government, tax, and conflict issues. I represented hundreds of churches and two regional denominations. I have been blessed to serve the church as a youth minister, deacon, elder, Sunday school teacher, Bible study leader, and presently as a commissioned minister. I believe in serving the church.

Sometimes the church needs help with tools in addressing legal, tax, government, and conflict issues. Administer Justice and Gospel Justice Initiative can provide guidance, direction, and counsel to connect the church with resources and individuals who can help. When the church has no resources and is poor itself, we can serve the church as one of our poor neighbors.

The pastor stood looking at the summons. The small, rural church had received funds from an estate for a number of years. The trust had been established by a farmer, who wanted to be certain the church adhered to biblical truth. So the trust included a clause requiring the church to adhere to the fundamental, evangelical tradition.

The church changed its name and left a denomination because that group was becoming liberal theologically. The lawsuit was seeking to remove the inheritance because the church was no longer the same church. Yet all the people remained the same, the pastor was the same, and the fundamental, evangelical doctrine remained the same.

The pastor thought he could just tell this to the other attorney and the judge—and the matter would be resolved. But when he went to court, the judge would not let him speak because he was not an attorney. The church could not address this injustice because they could not afford one. They needed an advocate. They found us.

We sought to address all those involved. We prayed for the judge, the opposing parties, and the opposing attorney. The case required a full trial before being resolved in the church's favor. The court victory was important for this small church—and carrying out the intent of the deceased farmer.

But just as important was the opportunity to minister to the opposing parties and the opposing attorney. The opposing counsel had grown up in a church but watched the church split and engage in bitter fighting. He left and had not returned.

Many people have been hurt by churches. Church leaders and church members are redeemed sinners. When we fail to reflect the character, compassion, and conduct of our Creator, we fail to understand how to live in community. We fall short.

Today I have an open invitation to have coffee and pray with the opposing counsel who thought the church was the enemy. When we administer true justice by showing compassion to our neighbors, we reflect our Lord and Savior.

ONE JERICHO ROAD

Your church is located at One Jericho Road. Whether God has placed you in a low-income neighborhood, a high-income neighborhood, a city, suburban, or rural area, wounded people live near you. The injustice of the Jericho Road affects us all.

Getting involved in justice for the needy is an opportunity to reflect God to our community. Will we make the most of this? Will we welcome a Samaritan—a lawyer—and a wounded sinner to our church?

Working together we can transform individuals and communities. Every community has needs. Every community has churches. Across the nation, churches join in the fight against injustice. Justice unites where other issues might divide. But first we must determine, "Is there room at the inn?"

CHAPTER 9

LESSONS FROM THE LAWYER

"The expert on the law answered, 'The one
who showed him mercy.'" —Luke 10:37 NCV

"Speak up for those who cannot speak for
themselves; ensure justice for those being crushed.
Yes, speak up for the poor and helpless,
and see that they get justice." —Proverbs 31:8–9 NLT

THE BOY HELD HIS father's hand as they walked across the cemetery lawn strewn with autumn leaves. He stopped and pulled on his father's arm. "Daddy."

"Yes, son."

"Why are there two men buried in this grave?"

The man looked and grinned. The epitaph read, "Here lies a lawyer and a Christian."

I first encountered the assumption behind this joke as a sixteen-year-old with a summer job at a restaurant, clearing tables and washing dishes. The owner was a Christian, and at my interview he asked what I planned to do after graduation. I said I wanted to be a lawyer. He looked surprised and said, "Young man, you cannot be a Christian and a lawyer."

The statement puzzled me. I worked hard all summer washing dishes, clearing tables, mopping floors, cleaning toilets, and doing whatever was needed. I chose not to engage with other employees in conversations that I knew were not appropriate, but neither did I avoid my fellow workers.

Some of the workers cut corners, asked friends to punch a time clock for them after they left, or helped themselves to food. I graciously challenged these activities. By the end of the summer the atmosphere at work had changed. The swearing and other activities had stopped.

My boss brought me into his office. He sized me up and shook his head. "I may be wrong," he said. "If anyone can be a Christian and a lawyer, I believe you can. Good luck, son."

Actions speak louder than words. The actions of some attorneys give rise to the belief you cannot be a lawyer and a Christian. The actions of the Samaritans over centuries had given rise to the belief that all Samaritans were evil. Certainly the lawyer in the parable did not believe the Samaritan could be godly.

The story was set in the question, "What must I do to inherit eternal life?" The answer was to love God first and then love your neighbor—His people, all people. That includes Samaritans. It even includes lawyers.

Unfortunately many lawyers struggle with whether they can be a lawyer and a Christian. They are not questioning their salvation, but the application of faith in the practice of law. Aren't they required to establish separate roles under the professional rules of conduct? Aren't they required to separate their head and their heart?

The lawyer who spoke with Jesus wrestled with this. He did not believe the Torah (his professional rules of conduct) would allow him to step outside his role to serve a Samaritan. The established view of the day supported his interpretation. Over the years the teachers of the law had become so enmeshed in thinking through the complexities of the law that they failed to grasp its weightier matters.

Jesus said to them, "And you experts in the law, woe to you, because you load people down with burdens they can hardly carry, and you yourselves will not lift one finger to help them" (Luke 11:46).

The teachers of the law failed to understand the interaction of law and justice. They saw only rules and retribution. Rather than burden the people, Jesus asked them to listen, learn, and sustain the weary. "The Sovereign Lord has given me an instructed tongue, to know the word that sustains the weary. He wakens me morning by morning, wakens my ear to listen like one being taught" (Isaiah 50:4).

Jesus asked the lawyers to use their instructed tongues to sustain the weary—and to listen and learn from Him. The parable of the Good Samaritan was told to this purpose. The lawyer was seeking to justify his knowledge of the law. Jesus wanted to engage his heart.

"Which of these three do you think was a neighbor to the man who fell into the hands of robbers?" Jesus asked.

The lawyer could not bring himself to use a word so distasteful as *Samaritan*, so he said, "The one who had mercy on him."

Did the lawyer transfer that knowledge to his hands and his heart? I don't know. Maybe the story transformed his view of the law and he became a follower of Jesus. Maybe he remained unmoved and marveled at how Jesus could twist the teachings of the Torah.

Jesus' question remains on the table. Will today's lawyers seek the weightier matters of the law—justice, mercy, and faithfulness—or will they focus on the rules, the complexities of the law, and miss the opportunity to administer true justice?

CHALLENGE ONE: THE HEAD
—LIES OF A DIVIDED LIFE

So what stops the lawyer? First is the struggle of the head. Some lawyers believe it is wrong to integrate faith and practice.

They can allow their faith to inform their actions, but they cannot demonstrate their faith overtly.

These lawyers have bought into the lie that when they walk into their office, they take off their Christian clothes and don neutral advocate clothing. Robed in these garments, they approach the client's position with complete dispassion—and zealous advocacy within the bounds of the law, or as far as they can stretch it.

Like Jesus, Job would challenge this divided life approach. He refused to put on neutral advocate robes, but "put on righteousness as my clothing; justice was my robe and my turban. I was eyes to the blind and feet to the lame. I was a father to the needy; I took up the case of the stranger. I broke the fangs of the wicked and snatched the victims from their teeth" (Job 29:14–17).

Job saw a person in need and used his influence to help. The Samaritan did the same. Jesus consistently commended such service—and consistently challenged the lawyers and Pharisees who refused to step outside of a narrow interpretation of the law to serve others.

The lawyers and Pharisees attacked Jesus for healing on the Sabbath, gathering grain on the Sabbath, and other activities that violated their view of the law. Lawyers today face a similar struggle. Under the standard paradigm some believe it is wrong to offer help in an area in which they are not an expert. For an estate planning attorney to assist a person with a foreclosure would violate their rules of professional conduct.

This is a lie. Not only is this contrary to our legal system's canon of ethics, it is directly contrary to the call of Christ.

Some lawyers justify not helping the poor by believing they are already doing such work when they are not paid by clients. Such thoughts are natural when we narrowly focus on the law, separate our identity, and fail to view our life in light of Christ's kingdom.

Recently there has been a push within the profession to ex-

amine a higher duty than one owed solely to the client. The higher
duty is owed to the government and court system.[1]

This is a duty of civic justice. While the Christians are called to
obey the authorities, they are not called to abandon their faith. Our
laws do not require us to do so. If they did, then like Peter we would
have to say, "We must obey God rather than men!" (Acts 5:29).

Questions of an attorney's role are prevalent in the profession. Administer Justice teaches an ethics seminar in which we
examine these roles in light of the accompanying paradigm chart.
The last two paradigms have been referred to as faith-informed
and faith-transformed,[2] or what we refer to as social justice and
gospel justice.

Social justice allows faith to inform the attorney's practice
through personal integrity and treating clients with respect. The focus is on the client's social welfare, while zealously advocating the client's interest. Faith inspires action, but is not transferred to the client.

Gospel justice is a faith-transformed model in which faith and
practice are inseparable. The focus is on the client's spiritual welfare,
in addition to the social welfare. This is a servant model in which
faith dialogue is encouraged as the means to provide true hope.

As Supreme Court Justice Benjamin Cardozo said, "Ethical
considerations can no more be excluded from the administration
of justice, which is the end and purpose of all civil laws, than one
can exclude the vital air from his room and live."[3]

Those ethical considerations include God's moral law. Attorney Gary Haugen, who leads International Justice Mission, takes
Cardozo's vital air analogy one step further. He says providing
practical help is like inhaling, and providing the hope of the gospel is like exhaling. You cannot do one without the other. "I don't
want to just exhale, I don't want to just inhale—I actually want to
breathe," Haugen says, "and that is what I think it means to love
our neighbor."[4]

Paradigms of a Lawyer's Role

	STANDARD PARADIGM	DUTY TO THE SYSTEM	FAITH–INFORMED DUTY	FAITH–TRANSFORMED DUTY
Lawyer's Role	Unfettered Advocate—Based on unfettered client loyalty and a strenuous advocacy of each client's cause presented by opposing lawyers to aneutral and passive decision maker.	Adviser and Advocate—Based on client loyalty tempered by lawyer's broader role as citizen and duty to the system.	Advocate—Will fight for client's rights to achieve substantial justice.	Advocate and Counselor—Counsel client in bigger picture including society and, as appropriate, faith.
Client's Role	While determining the desired outcome, the lawyer as champion decides all matters to accomplish.	Secondary to broader interest, at least in government arena.	Partner. Client has important value as a person. Treated like friend.	Child of God—Treated like someone who is loved by God regardless of their belief in God.
Lawyer-Client Relationship	Lawyer as Senior Partner using expert knowledge to do whatever is necessary within bounds of law to accomplish client's desired outcome.	Lawyer as Junior Partner using expert knowledge to advance client interest but subject to government/ societal duty that serves as senior partner.	Lawyer as associate working alongside client and desiring to help them with more than just legal but also social issues.	Lawyer as servant seeking to serve the client by demonstrating mercy and compassion as a counselor.
Role of System, Community, or Other Interested Parties	None. Lawyer answers only to client.	Important and necessary consideration.	Secondary to importance of justice for the client.	Important to empower client so client can escape cycles of conflict and learn new patterns for the future.
Role of Justice	Neutral. By-product of advocacy.	Civic Justice.	Social Justice.	Gospel Justice.
Desired Outcome	Win at all costs.	Maximum benefit for society and client.	Advance societal justice. Individual interest sometimes subservient to greater cause interest.	Transformation. Through permissive prayer and permissive spiritual dialogue to address all issues and involve a community.

Lawyers believe firmly in providing good comprehensive advice. But how can we love our neighbor and effectively serve the person across from us if we do not provide them *all* their options? This means providing an opportunity to consider God's role in a conflict—and what He might have for the client.

Ultimately the client must choose to accept God's plan or reject it—the same as they must accept the lawyer's plan concerning a legal issue or reject it. This is the faith-transformed model that reflects the heart of gospel justice.

Many lawyers cannot implement such a model because their employers prohibit such conduct. But Christian legal aid affords a unique opportunity for every lawyer to fully integrate faith and practice.

Al was a partner in a mid-sized Christian law practice. He had never prayed with a client. Although his firm advertised their personal Christian commitment, he was uncomfortable praying or engaging in spiritual discussion.

"I knew the first thing on the checklist (at an Administer Justice client appointment) was prayer," Al said, "but I wasn't comfortable doing that. Bruce encouraged me, and I decided to try. When I raised my head, tears were streaming down the face of the client. I could not help but be moved."

That scene is replayed at our office several times a day, six days a week. As another volunteer attorney says, "There's an incredible ability to mirror Christ's love in the world in interacting with other people on His behalf because of what He has done for us."

Al's practice was transformed. He received training in conflict coaching so he could better address conflict and the gospel in client meetings. He began incorporating this into his private law practice, and his entire career changed.

CHALLENGE TWO: THE HAND
—LIES OF BUSYNESS

The second challenge attorneys face is that we become so busy, we lose sight of God's plan for us. Many professionals begin their careers because they want to make a difference. Full of dreams, they are ready to take the world by a storm. Then somewhere along the way, the notion of justice fades. In its place, the law becomes a jealous mistress.

Time is a lawyer's stock and trade. They face great pressure to produce billable hours. Many live on a six-minute or fifteen-minute clock by which they must account for their activities. Outside of work, lawyers are often called to serve on church and organization boards. At church, social gatherings, and other venues they are often bombarded with legal questions.

The law becomes their life. Even at home lawyers find it hard to not think about the challenges of their profession. Others wrestle with guilt as they feel torn between the demands of family and career. This is the work of our adversary, who wants to keep us so distracted, we cannot make a difference.

Don't be fooled. Being BUSY often means "Being Under Satan's Yoke." God created us to make a difference.

Lawyers have an incredible capacity to do that. The most recent study conducted by the Legal Services Corporation, just before the 2007 recession, revealed that for every client served by a legal service corporation-funded program, at least one person who sought help was turned away because of insufficient resources.[5]

Fewer than one in five legal problems experienced by low-income people are addressed with the assistance of either a private attorney (*pro bono* or paid) or a legal aid lawyer.[6] This often leads to tragic circumstances which undercut the very fabric of our democracy.

One hundred years ago, Harvard University commissioned

attorney Reginald Heber Smith with the task of identifying the challenges of the legal system toward the poor and methods for addressing these challenges. One of the chief conclusions was the critically important role of the lawyer: "The lawyer is indispensable to the conduct of the proceedings before the courts, and yet the fees which he must charge for his services are more than millions of persons can pay."[7]

Smith's conclusion to Harvard was, "the machinery of justice can be operated only through attorneys, that attorneys must be paid for their services, and that the poor are unable to pay for such services. This is the great, the inherent, and fundamental difficulty—inherent because our legal institutions were framed with the intention that trained advocates should be employed, and fundamental in the sense that no amount of reorganization or simplification, short of a complete overturn of the whole structure, can entirely remove the necessity for the attorney."[8]

Without effective assistance of counsel, there can be no justice. We attorneys must not allow our business or the busyness of law to cause us to forget that we are ministers of justice.

CHALLENGE THREE: THE HEART
—LIES OF LIMITED RESOURCES

The third great challenge is developing a heart for justice. Our pastor friends tell us the best indicator of our spiritual health is to look at our checkbook and our calendar. Jesus said the same to the lawyers of his day. "Woe to you, teachers of the law and Pharisees, you hypocrites! You give a tenth of your spices—mint, dill and cumin. But you have neglected the more important matters of the law—justice, mercy and faithfulness. You should have practiced the latter, without neglecting the former" (Matthew 23:23).

We should spend our time executing justice and mercy while providing the support of our time and money. That was the point

Jesus made to the lawyer in the parable. The lawyer was to be like the Samaritan and give of his time and resources to combat injustice and demonstrate mercy.

The Samaritan was busy. He had not planned on donating two days' wages and promising more if needed. He could have rationalized that his resources were limited, and chosen to keep his time and his money. But he chose mercy over money.

> THE SAMARITAN HAD NOT PLANNED ON DONATING TWO DAYS' WAGES AND PROMISING MORE IF NEEDED.

The most current statistics reveal that private attorneys give less than 1 percent of their time to help the poor[9]—and an average annual donation of only $276.[10] Many do more, but as a profession this highlights the significant need for legal-aid attorneys and the financial support of Christian Legal Aid. We have a historic opportunity to recapture the heart of our profession.

The first code of ethics in America for lawyers stated: "I shall never close my ear or heart because my clients' means are low. Those who have none, and who have just causes, are, of all others, the best entitled to sue or be defended; and they shall receive a due portion of my services, cheerfully given."[11]

In 1884 our professional ethics provided: "It is indeed the noblest faculty of the profession to counsel the ignorant, defend the weak and oppressed, and to stand forth on all occasions as the bulwark of private rights against the assaults of power."[12]

One hundred years ago we were referred to as ministers of justice. We can be again.

She came storming into the office. "I's got to see me the minister of justice. Where is the minister of justice?"

Her question was profound. Like many, she was mispronouncing our name—Administer Justice. I appreciate the error, as I hope it reflects a deeper truth.

Thelma was a large, African-American woman. She was upset with the injustice of her community, which was riddled with crime, fraud, and abuse. She wanted to fight back, but the neighborhood lacked the financial resources to hire an attorney.

We helped her form a community association to provide a forum for residents to discuss the injustices and plan a way to address them. The group would seek legal guidance from time to time as they worked to make a difference.

Every year more than one million low-income people in this country cry out to see a minister of justice. One by one they are turned away because of a lack of resources. Nearly three times that number need help, but assume none is available and don't even look. Where is the minister of justice?

The word *minister* means agent, and as a minister of justice we are charged with delivering justice. "Speak up for those who cannot speak for themselves, for the rights of all who are destitute. Speak up and judge fairly; defend the rights of the poor and needy" (Proverbs 31:8–9).

Attorneys, especially Christian attorneys, are uniquely qualified to serve as ministers of justice. By virtue of our profession we have a special duty to serve. While this call is for all, it does not mean all will serve full-time. Like missionaries, only a few will be called to full-time service. And like missionaries, those men and women need financial and volunteer support.

Every Christian lawyer can spend some time serving on this mission field, for which he is distinctly qualified. Only the lawyer can speak in the halls of justice. Only the lawyer can render legal advice.

You have a unique call to administer justice. Still doubt? Have

you ever used the post nominal of our profession—*esq.* or *esquire?*
The word means "shield bearer." You are a shield bearer in the fight
against injustice. Take up the shield of faith and join the battle.

FOLLOW JESUS TO THE POOR

What prevents you from living up to your calling? Time, expertise, station of life, fear, pride—all can be justice-robbers. Like
the priest and the Levite, we miss the opportunity.

Jesus warned people about the teachers of the law. "They like
to walk around in flowing robes and love to be greeted in the mar-
ketplaces, and have the most important seats in the synagogues
and the places of honor at banquets. They devour widows' houses
and for a show make lengthy prayers. Such men will be punished
most severely" (Luke 20:46–47).

By focusing on themselves instead of the poor, they missed the
opportunity to prevent the foreclosure of the widows' home.

Mother Teresa was once asked, "How did you receive your call
to serve the poor?" She answered, "My call is not to serve the poor.
My call is to follow Jesus. I have followed Him to the poor."[13]

Follow Jesus to the poor. Pam did.

Pam had been an attorney for many years, but not used her
license. She worked in the computer industry until she lost her
job in the economic downturn. Deciding to return to law, she volunteered with us to sharpen her skills. She never expected God
would use her to do much more.

Jane came storming into the office, wanting to pursue her
employer for wrongfully terminating her. Because Illinois is an
employment-at-will state, and she had already lost two hearings,
pursuing an action would not have been in Jane's best interest. The
legal issue was straightforward, but we don't serve issues, we serve
people. Pam listened, prayed, and encouraged Jane. Jane wrote back:

> You gave me sound advice, and the Christian help was especially appreciated. Pam took the time to go over everything in detail and explain why she didn't feel this was worth my while. The part that especially resonated with me was when Pam shared some of her own experiences and even recommended a book, *When Life Is Hard.* . . . I can't thank Pam enough!

Follow Jesus to the poor, and He will provide you with all you need to make a difference. That is what Jeff did.

Jeff is a successful attorney in a large employment firm in Chicago. From his offices overlooking Lake Michigan, he doesn't see many poor people. He was active in church and wanted to help people, but had little thought of helping the poor.

He agreed to volunteer at one of our Saturday morning four-hour legal appointments because his friend asked him.

"On that first Saturday I was pretty nervous," Jeff says. "I was nervous that I would be useless to the people who came for help. I didn't know anything about family law; I never even took that class in law school, and that had been a long time ago."

Ten years have passed, and Jeff still regularly volunteers with us. He no longer does this for his friend, but for himself and the clients. As he says,

> I do it for the clients, because I learned that with God's help, I can help them. At the beginning of every client session I explain that I am a volunteer, that I don't concentrate in the area of law of their need, and probably won't be able to answer all of their questions, but that I can help get them on the right path. I can listen to their issues and help formulate a plan to resolve them. Sometimes, the plan is to refer them to an attorney for representation, sometimes

it is sufficient to direct them to someone for specific legal counseling about how to address their specific issue, and sometimes it is explaining that their issue is not a "legal" issue, but something else entirely.

The other thing I do at the beginning of every meeting is to explain that I am a *Christian* volunteer and ask their permission to start with prayer. And then I do. I ask God to help me, to help me understand the situation, and to give me wisdom. When there is tension or high emotions, I ask for God's peace.

. . . In every instance I have felt God working in the meetings. I could sense His presence, His peace, and His compassion. In every instance, even though I am not a poverty lawyer, God gave me what I needed to know to be able to help the clients in their circumstances. Answered prayers build faith, and my service with Administer Justice has done that for me.

Jeff's experience is common. As attorneys use their unique gifts to serve the poor, their faith is expanded. For most it is an ever-present reminder of God's blessing in their life. As Jeff says:

When I meet with people with problems, it is impossible for me not to recognize that "there but for the grace of God go I." Sometimes the clients did nothing to cause their problems—the problems were the result of health issues, accidents, or even the bad choices of others. Sometimes the problems were the consequences of their own decisions, but similar decisions to ones I have made. All of this has shown me that I am blessed, and that it is not because of what I have done, but because of what God has done for me.

Mike returned to law after many years working in the airline industry as a pilot. He was looking for some experience, and a friend told him about our office. While he faced struggles in starting a practice and had some health issues, they paled with the needs of the clients he encountered.

Manuel came into the office tired, angry, and impatient. He told a story that was hard to believe. His girlfriend had died in childbirth. His infant daughter, Sandra, had lost oxygen when her mother died and suffered brain damage. Manuel had not been identified as the father on the birth certificate, so the hospital would not allow him to make decisions on Sandra's behalf.

Based on Manual's appearance and demeanor, Mike thought the story was a scam for services. But he took the information and scheduled another appointment. Afterward Mike called the hospital, which confirmed the mother had died and that Manual was tirelessly by the baby's side. His emotions were raw from grief and lack of sleep. The hospital had referred him to us for help.

Mike was overwhelmed. How could something so tragic be true? Manual hadn't looked like a devoted father, and Mike had wrongly judged him.

Mike gladly prepared the forms to help Manual and talked him through every step. Today Sandra remains hospitalized. But she has a legal father, and her dad can see her, is involved in her health-care decisions, and from time to time can take Sandra home with him for short stays.

"I have to be careful not to judge," Mike says. "I need to count my blessings every day. I am so grateful to use the gifts God has given me to make a difference."

ALLOW GRACE TO MAKE YOU JUST

"If a person has grasped the meaning of God's grace in his heart, he will do justice," Pastor Tim Keller writes in his book

Generous Justice. "If he doesn't live justly, then he may say with his lips that he is grateful for God's grace, but in his heart he is far from him. If he doesn't care about the poor, it reveals at best he doesn't understand the grace he has experienced, and at worst he has not really encountered the saving mercy of God. Grace should make you just."[14]

Have you experienced God's grace in your life? When we fully embrace the truth that we are all lawbreakers who deserve eternal separation from God, we cannot help but demonstrate justice, mercy, and compassion toward others. And as we do, how can we not share the truth that set us free?

Salvation is a gift to be shared. That person across from you needs to know that God loves them, died for them, and is willing to forgive them if they will acknowledge their failure and invite Him to become Lord of their life. This is good news!

You are a minister of justice. You are humbly offering a free gift you cannot force them to take. But how can they make the choice if you do not offer it?

Theresa received her law degree but never practiced. She was blessed to stay home and raise her two children. After her children were grown, she read a book, *The Body* by Chuck Colson, and knew she must share what God had so graciously given to her. A friend told her about us, and five years later she still comes in three days a week to make a difference.

Liz graduated from law school later in life. She loves using her law degree to serve others. "I live to give back to Him," she says.

Mark was a successful businessman but was getting bored with his routine. He felt an attraction to the law and attended law school in his early fifties. After graduating he wondered how he could use his degree. Someone at church suggested volunteering at our office.

"I came face-to-face with people who needed real help but

lacked the resources to hire an attorney," Mark says. "On the personal level, once I became involved with it and started meeting with clients, I was struck by the incredible need."

Mark's first client was Felipe, a young Spanish-speaking father who received a final warning from the IRS saying that unless he came in within 90 days, his wages would be garnished and liens would be placed on his property. Felipe, who had dutifully paid his taxes, was having his refund withheld because of unreported income from a company he never worked for. Someone was using his identification number, and those earnings were being reported to the IRS as having been earned by Felipe.

Mark filed in tax court and persuaded the government that Felipe could not have worked in two different places at the same time. His $5,000 tax obligation was wiped clean—and for this laborer with a wife and four children, that was an enormous burden lifted.

"No one has ever stood up for me before," Felipe says. "I will never forget what he did for me."

Mark volunteers regularly, although the cases are still outside his comfort zone. "There's no question that most of us are outside our comfort zones on a lot of these subjects, and that's a scary thing for lawyers." But he sees that as a small price to pay for the opportunity to serve as a witness of Christ's love to people in deep need.

Ann agrees. She is a municipal attorney with no experience in poverty issues, but an encounter on a Saturday morning changed her life. "I truly feel it is my calling to help the clients that Administer Justice serves, and I would love to make it my life's work."

SUPPORTING ZENAS

Nearly every week we hear from an attorney who wants to make this their life's work. They would give up significant income to make a difference, but they don't know how and they need resources. These missionaries need support. Like Zenas of New Testament days, they can make a significant difference with the support of the church, individuals, and a national network.

Zenas was a lawyer who traveled with Apollos and was commended by Paul to Titus: "Do everything you can to help Zenas the lawyer and Apollos on their way and see that they have everything they need" (Titus 3:13).

Christians need to see that lawyers have everything they need to serve the poor. One way to help is through prayer. Instead of criticizing lawyers, let's pray for them. We can also provide financial support of a national association that can train, encourage, equip, and provide grants for lawyers to serve the poor. Administer Justice and Gospel Justice Initiative have the tools to equip lawyers so they can serve others.

> INSTEAD OF CRITICIZING LAWYERS, LET'S PRAY FOR THEM.

Our prayer is that thousands like Zenas will be armed to provide help and hope. Hope is Administer Justice's pledge, which we emphasize with every volunteer. HOPE is an acronym for Help, Overcome, Plan, and Empower.

We provide help to all who come, regardless of their race, religion, ethnicity, or any other status except that they are low-income. We ask our attorneys to seek help even as they offer help—to see the client appointment as a divine appointment and to ask themselves what the Lord has in store for this encounter. This requires active listening.

As we listen, we recognize we are sinners in need of grace. We do not come in as professionals with perfect answers. We come in as Samaritans loving our neighbor. And that means we holistically help our neighbor overcome barriers. Each client needs to know that God is not absent; He has a plan for their lives, a plan to offer hope and a future. They matter to God, and they matter to us.

Each client receives an individualized plan that includes specific next steps, area church referrals, area resources, and a prayer card to let them know we are praying for them. The plan is different for each person because each person is different.

Finally, each attorney seeks to empower those who come. Many clients want someone to do everything for them. We believe in having them take action on their own behalf to the extent possible. This way they learn how to resolve issues and recognize that, with some help, they can do more than they thought. This is also why we charge a $20 administrative fee (the only fee charged clients). The fee is not a means to make money, but a way to overcome a something-for-nothing mentality.

Ultimately such empowerment reflects the life-changing power available through the Holy Spirit. The Spirit does not do everything for us or automatically make life easy. Rather the Spirit teaches us that by learning the truths of Scripture, we can overcome life's challenges—and in the process be conformed to the image of Jesus Christ.

YOU CAN MAKE A DIFFERENCE

We pledge to defend the cause of the poor and helpless through legal help and gospel hope. You can join in that mission. You can make a difference.

Whether you serve four or forty hours, you can make a profound difference.

Training will better equip you to meet practical legal needs while providing eternal hope. But don't let the fear of stepping outside your comfort zone stop you.

Whenever I speak to lawyers I tell them that, after serving tens of thousands of clients, I have never had a client write and thank us for the attorney's legal brilliance. But every day we receive letters thanking lawyers for their prayers, their compassion, and concern.

This is not about your head, but your heart and your hands. Use your gifts to serve the poor and see how God transforms your heart as you serve His people.

One day we will die. Time is the great equalizer—we all have the same amount of it in a given day, and none of us knows how many days we have been given. Let's live like Job, with one eye on eternity and the other on serving the poor.

> If I have denied justice to my menservants and maidservants when they had a grievance against me, what will I do when God confronts me? What will I answer when called to account? Did not he who made me in the womb make them? Did not the same one form us both within our mothers? If I have denied the desires of the poor or let the eyes of the widow grow weary, if I have kept my bread to myself, not sharing it with the fatherless—but from my youth I reared him as would a father, and from my birth I guided the widow—if I have seen anyone perishing for lack of clothing, or a needy man without a garment, and his heart did not bless me for warming him with the fleece from my sheep, if I have raised my hand against the fatherless, knowing that I had influence in court, then let my arm fall from the shoulder, let it be broken off at the joint. (Job 31:13–22)

One day we will all give an account to God. As you picture yourself arriving at the pearly gates, imagine Peter asking you to stand in a receiving line along with Daniel, Esther, and other great men and women of the faith. As you stand there with these heroes of the faith, person after person stops to thank you for sharing the faith and leading them to the Lord.

They thank you for praying with them and letting them know God loves them, which placed them on a path that led to their salvation. They thank you for making a difference in the most difficult hours of their life. Overwhelmed, you see Jesus look at you, smile, and say, "Well done, my good and faithful servant."

CHAPTER 10

LESSONS FROM JESUS

"Jesus told him, 'Go and do likewise.'" —Luke 10:37

"Therefore everyone who hears these words of mine
and puts them into practice is like a wise man who
built his house on the rock." —Matthew 7:24

JERUSALEM WAS ABUZZ. "Did you see the crowds when Jesus entered yesterday?" "They say Jesus will be king." "I heard Jesus makes the blind see." "Jesus is coming here from Bethany." "Maybe we'll get to see Jesus perform a miracle."

The name electrified the air. Many made their way through the temple's court of the Gentiles, using it as a shortcut from the Mount of Olives. The temple court bustled with merchants selling birds and animals for the Passover.

As the people longed for a king to free them from Rome, they saw the money exchangers trading Roman currency for the temple coinage. Even as they hoped to see miracles, they saw Gentiles trying to pray amid the noise and smell of animals.

They saw, but they did not see. They were thinking of Jesus. They were thinking of the greatness they might see. They wanted change—and believed Jesus could bring it. Focused on what that would mean for them, they marched past the injustice among them.

Jesus was coming. The air was tense with anticipation. But today Jesus would not enter on a colt to the crowd's praise. Today He would shock the people. His popularity would evaporate. Jesus wasn't who they wanted Him to be. Even now He stood before the city, resolute in what He must do.

Jesus examined a fig tree in full leaf. The disciples thought it strange He should look for fruit out of season. They were surprised when He got angry and cursed the tree, which would wither and die. Not seeing what Jesus saw, they failed to understand.

Jesus knew what awaited in Jerusalem. While His heart wept for the lost (Luke 19:41), it burned against the proud. He knew the hearts of people who looked good on the outside, but bore no fruit. The fig tree served as an illustration of fruitless lives. Without another word, He set out for the temple.

Entering the court of the Gentiles, He ignored the whispers of staring people. He was glaring at the injustice they ignored. Poor pilgrims were being robbed. Merchants were taking advantage of them as they needed an offering for the Passover. The money lenders used dishonest scales to exploit the poor. Jesus responded in righteous anger. (See Matthew 21:12–13, Mark 11:15–17, Luke 19:45–46.)

"Crack!" The sound of a whip shattered the noise of people and animals. Those gathered around Jesus fled as coins went flying, merchants scattered, cages burst, and birds took to the air. An angry voice cried out, "My house will be called a house of prayer for all nations, but you have made it a den of robbers" (Mark 11:17).

Jesus intentionally quoted Isaiah and Jeremiah.

The Isaiah passage began, "Be just and fair to all. Do what is right and good, for I am coming soon to rescue you and to display my righteousness among you" (Isaiah 56:1 NLT).

Do what is right and good. Be just and fair to all. Jesus is coming to rescue and display His righteousness in anger against those who exploit others.

Jeremiah called the temple a den of robbers because the people exploited foreigners, orphans, and widows:

> ... don't be fooled by those who promise you safety simply because the Lord's Temple is here ... But I will be merciful only if you stop your evil thoughts and deeds and start treating each other with justice; only if you stop exploiting foreigners, orphans, and widows. (Jeremiah 7:4–6 NLT)

Jesus could not abide injustice. He refused to stand by while people were exploited. The lesson of Jesus is that He got engaged and enraged in the face of injustice. He took action. He commands us to do the same, to "go and do likewise."

GO—GET ENGAGED

Jesus engaged with the poor and oppressed. He worked for His coming kingdom and taught His disciples to follow His example.

> I have set you an example that you should do as I have done for you. I tell you the truth, no servant is greater than his master, nor is a messenger greater than the one who sent him. Now that you know these things, you will be blessed if you do them. (John 13:15–17)

What did Jesus do? He washed feet. Three days after clearing the temple, He knelt in an upper room demonstrating love and humility as He washed the feet of His friends. "You are my friends if you do what I command" (John 15:14).

What did Jesus command? "A new command I give you: Love one another. As I have loved you, so you must love one another" (John 13:34).

Love requires action. If you say you love someone but never demonstrate it, your love is not real. Love compels us to wash the feet and wounds of our friend and neighbor on the Jericho Road. Jesus so engaged humanity that He sacrificed His own life to redeem us.

That day in the temple, the authorities determined they could no longer allow Jesus to live. He claimed the temple was His house—that He was God. He claimed He was greater than the temple: "Destroy this temple, and I will raise it again in three days" (John 2:19).

Such blasphemy could not go unpunished. Within three days they negotiated a betrayal and a series of unjust trials.

Jesus walked the Jericho Road, the Via Dolorosa, the way of suffering. He took our sin upon Himself. He suffered a cruel and unjust death on a Roman instrument of torture between two common thieves.

The temple authorities should have been gloating over their victory, but the perpetrators of injustice reacted in fear. They pleaded with Pilate for a large stone to be placed over the tomb entrance. They understood Jesus' words about rising in three days—and were afraid. They thought the official seal and guards at the tomb would save them.

Death could not contain the High King of heaven. The great stone of injustice was rolled away, and justice rolled on in its place. Jesus willingly suffered the greatest injustice so He could freely offer the greatest justice. He engaged with humanity. He showed us how to love our neighbor victimized by sin and injustice. That love compels us to go and do likewise.

Jesus said, "Therefore everyone who hears these words of mine and puts them into practice is like a wise man who built his house on the rock. The rain came down, the streams rose, and the winds blew and beat against that house; yet it did not fall, because it had its foundation on the rock" (Matthew 7:24–25).

We are called to be people of action. We are called to be members of the Lord's army battling sin and injustice. Get engaged. Get involved. Make a difference.

GO—GET ENRAGED

Art and movies often distort our view of Jesus. Jesus was not weak. Too often we believe that being like Jesus means we do our best to be kind and honest. We go along and get along. That is a distortion.

Jesus challenged the status quo. He stood for truth in an age that asked, "What is truth?" (John 18:38).

The teachers of the law and Pharisees twisted the truth to their own ends. That enraged Jesus. He called them "whitewashed tombs," a "brood of vipers," "hypocrites," and "blind guides" (Matthew 12:34; 23:16, 27). Jesus pointed to their actions and said, "Do not do what they do, for they do not practice what they preach" (Matthew 23:3).

Truth cannot abide evil. Truth cannot ignore injustice. Truth is found in Jesus, and as we follow Jesus we work for the coming kingdom. When Jesus returns as King He will do so in fire and glory. The image of Jesus in Revelation is not of someone

> TRUTH CANNOT ABIDE EVIL. TRUTH CANNOT IGNORE INJUSTICE.

weak. He is a conquering King coming to cast evil from the world and establish a reign of justice and righteousness.

If we are to follow Jesus, we must not abide evil. We must not ignore injustice. We must administer *true* justice. We must respond to the effects of sin with love and grace toward the wounded—and strong resolve toward the systems and individuals that oppress them.

The stories in this book should evoke response. Our modern widow, fatherless, alien, and poor are being deprived justice.

Does it bother you that elderly residents are frequently victims of financial exploitation and physical abuse? They need advocates to intervene in health care issues, guardianships, estate matters,

Medicare/Medicaid, and identity theft.

Are you upset that fatherless children comprise the greatest percentage of poor in this country? Does it bother you that many children bounce from home to home, sleeping on floors or in basements? They need advocates so they can stay in their school with friends. They need child support. They need guardianships. They deserve stability.

Are you concerned about the foreigner among us who faces unfair wages or no wages, financial exploitation in loans and tax returns, domestic slavery, sexual exploitation, and physical abuse? These individuals need advocates to cut through the legal and government systems to provide hope and justice.

Can you feel the weight of the poor who encounter legal or government issues for which they cannot receive help? These involve:

▸ family issues (divorce, domestic violence, support, guardianships)
▸ housing (foreclosure, uninhabitable tenements, evictions)
▸ consumer issues (fraud, deceptive practices, small claims)
▸ employment (unemployment, discrimination)
▸ many other issues including tax, immigration, Social Security disability, government benefits, bankruptcy, and schooling

These result in great stress, fear, and feelings of helplessness.

Some of us misplace our anger. We are bothered by these matters, but blame the victim. We must look to Jesus and the Word of God. God cares about justice for the widow, the fatherless, the alien, and the poor. Jesus was criticized for loving sinners. Jesus knew that broken, hurting people were open to the message of salvation and change.

We have unprecedented opportunity to demonstrate justice, mercy, and compassion. Dare to get engaged and enraged in the battle for justice.

TAKE THE INITIATIVE

We need advocates to defend the rights of the poor and help-less. We advocate because Christ advocates for us.

I am writing this to you so that you will not sin. But if any-one does sin, *we have an advocate who pleads our case before the Father.* He is Jesus Christ, the one who is truly righ-teous. He himself is the sacrifice that atones for our sins—and not only our sins but the sins of all the world. And we can be sure that we know him if we obey his command-ments. If someone claims, "I know God," but doesn't obey God's commandments, that person is a liar and is not living in the truth. But those who obey God's word truly show how completely they love him. That is how we know we are living in him. Those who say they live in God should live their lives as Jesus did. (1 John 2:1–6 NLT, emphasis added)

Live as Jesus did. Don't just be hearers of the Word, but do what it commands. Get involved. Take the initiative.

John Robb helped lead the charge before Congress in the 1970s for legal help for the poor. Twenty years later, through a national effort with Christian Legal Society, he was leading the charge for gospel hope along with legal help. As good as those efforts were, he felt God calling him to a massive expansion of Christian legal aid groups around the country. He believed there could be a thousand such groups—and that the impact would transform churches and communities. John was in his eighties when he received this vision. The call is for all, no matter what our station in life.

Shortly after John began work in this new effort, I felt the same need to excite and equip those who felt God's call to advo-cate for the poor and helpless. God brought John and me together, and for more than a year we met weekly by phone to pray and seek God's direction. We brought together leaders from Administer Justice, those in legal aid, church leaders, and individuals from across the nation to fast and pray. The result was the formation of Gospel Justice Initiative.

Gospel Justice Initiative provides churches, ministries, individuals, and attorneys with the tools they need to take the initiative in being an advocate. Together we can make an eternal difference in the lives of hundreds of thousands of people.

Like the lawyer in the parable of the Good Samaritan, we have a choice. Will we get enraged and engaged? Will we advocate for the gospel and justice? Or will we blindly walk past the opportunity? Twelve ordinary men changed the world because they chose to believe Jesus. They went and did likewise. So can you. Here's how.

HOW TO ENTER THE BATTLE FOR JUSTICE: GET EDUCATED

Study the needs in your community. Understand the battlefield where you are called to serve. Gospel Justice Initiative (www.gji. org) maintains statistics of need, as does the US Census.[1] Spend time listening to your community. Serve in outreach ministries in your church and spend time listening to the needs of your neighbors. Do this as a group with your Bible study or friends.

If you do not have such ministries in your church, visit a low-income service provider in your area. Go to Senior Services, the Salvation Army, Union Gospel Mission, or another provider. Talk to the directors and ask what systemic issues they encounter.

Take a field trip to your courthouse and watch the proceedings. This is another good group activity. You will immediately see the challenges faced by individuals caught in the system. Ask to meet with the chief judge to learn about the challenges faced by unrepresented individuals. Most judges are happy to come speak to a group, as they want to encourage community involvement. You can also do this with your state representative and senator. They will know many of the needs, and you will find them receptive to discussions about helping the community.

Study the Bible. Use this book, any of the books cited here, a word study on *justice,* or a book study of James. Raise the awareness of others and engage them in the dialogue. Visit gji.org for more information.

Learn the needs of our modern widow, fatherless, alien, and poor. For widows, do an Internet search on *financial exploitation* and *elder abuse*. For the fatherless, search *homeless children*. For the alien, search *immigrant exploitation* or *trafficking*. For the poor, search *legal needs of the poor*. You may be shocked to learn the depth of need in America, and the lack of resources.

Host a "Justice Sunday." Gospel Justice Initiative has a kit for you to use including video, facts, and biblical references. Encourage attorneys to use their gifts in a unique service opportunity with the church. Involve others to help existing ministries in the community. Demonstrate the difference the gospel makes for lives in need of help and hope.

GET INVOLVED

Pray. Once you know the needs, begin to pray regularly for them. Pray for wisdom in how you might address the needs, pray for others to join you, and pray for the hearts of all those involved. Sign up for the Gospel Justice Initiative monthly prayer calendar so you can also pray for others engaged in the battle across the nation.

Prayer is our greatest weapon in the battle against injustice. Do not think of it as perfunctory. Prayer moves mountains that cannot be moved by human effort.

Get going. Start by examining what you have learned. Look at the service ministries in your church or community and seek common threads of need. Pull together a planning group and establish a goal. Make it specific.

For example: "By the end of the year we will launch a gospel justice center alongside our children's ministry to educate and advocate for the needs of homeless children in our school district."

Brainstorm ways to connect needs and ministries and work together toward a comprehensive solution. Design a program and determine what will be needed to make it successful. Evaluate your objectives and actions for effective impact.

Get help. While you must determine the specific area of need to address and how to coordinate existing services, we have the tools to launch an effective gospel justice ministry. Become a member of Gospel Justice Initiative and receive access to resources, best practices, an online database and volunteer coordination tool, educational resources, highly competent staff, an ability to dialogue with others for encouragement and support, ongoing training, and educational conferences.

Become an advocate. Get trained and get involved. Then involve others. Together you will make a difference.

GET GIVING

Give thanks. As you enter the world of injustice, you will recognize the blessings of God poured out upon you by His grace. You have significant resources compared to many others. You have been spared the tragedy of others, or perhaps you have experienced them but God has restored you. Each breath you take is a gift from God. Thank Him for it.

The natural expression of our salvation is to worship God and give Him thanks. That thanks will find expression in serving the victim of injustice on the Jericho Road. By getting involved, we reflect the love of Christ to a world in need.

"This service that you perform is not only supplying the needs of God's people but is also overflowing in many expressions of thanks to God. Because of the service by which you have proved yourselves, men will praise God for the obedience that accompanies your confession of the gospel of Christ, and for your generosity in sharing with them and with everyone else" (2 Corinthians 9:12–13).

Give time. There is no substitute for stopping on the Jericho Road to make a difference. Not only you but your whole family can engage in this ministry. You do not have to travel halfway around the world. You can invest whatever time you have to make a difference together.

Whether being trained as an attorney, financial counselor, or conflict coach, or serving by helping someone complete information, praying with someone, baking cookies, typing, calling, or in numerous other ways great or small, you can make a difference.

Give money. There is no better way to demonstrate your concern than to financially support the fight against injustice.

As a family you can study the needs together and give toward this work. Have your kids raise awareness among their friends about the plight of homeless children. Have them do an activity to raise support. Be creative. For ideas, visit www.gji.org.

Are you a businessman? Consider posting a sign or decal

in your business demonstrating your support of Gospel Justice Initiative.

Host an awareness lunch. Bring an attorney from your local Gospel Justice Center to educate workers on issues of importance to them, such as elder law issues their parents are likely to face, wills and powers of attorney, immigration, homelessness, or other topics relevant to your community.

Like the Samaritan who gave two days' wages to restore the victim of injustice, consider sacrificing two days' gross profits as a donation to Gospel Justice Initiative, which supports work in local communities.

Is your church looking to get involved, but has no access to attorneys? Take the Samaritan challenge and provide two days' support for the fight against injustice. Contact Gospel Justice Initiative to see if there are resources nearby you can partner with.

As an individual, consider taking the same Samaritan challenge. As the Lord leads, give two days of your gross wages to invest in gospel justice.

While secular legal aid provides important services, those are significantly incomplete. They are unable to reach a significant number of clients, and they are prohibited from addressing systemic issues and from helping certain classes of people, including the alien. Most importantly, they offer no eternal hope.

We have an unprecedented opportunity to do significantly more at a fraction of the cost spent by the government. Christians can demonstrate to a watching world the difference Christ makes.

In the Old Testament, landowners were required to support the widow, the fatherless, the alien, and the poor separate from their tithe. As author Amber Van Schooneveld says:

> The law of gleaning was up to each individual landowner, and I wonder what that means for my life . . . It can be

easy to rely on our government systems or church tithes to provide for the poor. But could this law of gleaning on top of tithing mean intentionally leaving aside a certain amount of my "crop" for those in need, even if my taxes and tithe are already supporting social welfare? I'm challenged to think that taking care of those in need isn't just a government or church concern, but also *my* personal concern.[2]

Loving our neighbor is our concern. We dare not be so busy or judgmental that we miss a divine opportunity to make a difference. Our support can change lives.

We serve a God of second chances. Give a second chance to someone in need.

GO AND DO LIKEWISE

Envision yourself in the crowd as Jesus told the story of those encounters along the Jericho Road. You'd been on your way to the market when you went to see what the commotion was about. You saw a teacher of the law stop that young traveling rabbi. Earlier today you had little concern outside of your to-do list. But something about Jesus caught your attention.

You heard the Great Question: "Teacher, what must I do to inherit eternal life?" The answer was worth hearing. Then came the Great Command: "Love the Lord your God with all your heart and with all your soul and with all your strength and with all your mind and love your neighbor as yourself."

Then came the Great Story. Strange and compelling as the young rabbi described the scene with such detail you could see the injured man, the Levite, the priest, and the Samaritan.

The very air was heavy as each listener understood the gravity of what the teacher was saying. Like the others, you understood the neighbor was the one who stood against injustice. The neighbor showed mercy. The neighbor got involved and sacrificed time and money and risked ridicule.

No one spoke. Even the birds seemed to go silent as the teacher looked first to the lawyer, then to all those present, and said, "Go and do likewise." Piercing eyes looked into your very soul as the words lingered in the still air.

Would you return to your grocery list?

Somehow the market seemed insignificant. Somehow your to-do's just don't seem as important.

You make a decision.

You run back to tell your family about your encounter with the rabbi who spoke such profound truth. You will go. You will make a difference. As you turn, you see the rabbi smile, and you know you have made the right decision.

NOTES

Introduction: Where Is Justice?

1. Approximately 31.6 percent of the population had at least one spell of poverty lasting two or more months during the four-year period from 2004 to 2007. Carmen DeNavas-Walt, Bernadette D. Proctor, and Jessica C. Smith, *U.S. Census Bureau, Current Population Reports*, 60-238; *Income, Poverty, and Health Insurance Coverage in the United States: 2009*, U.S. Government Printing Office, Washington D.C. 2010, 4.

2. 44.4 percent of children under age 18, and 54.3 percent of children under the age of 6 living with a single mom were living in poverty—four times the rate of children living in married-couple families (11 and 13.4 percent). Ibid., 15–16.

3. Bill Hybels, *The Power of a Whisper* (Grand Rapids: Zondervan, 2010).

4. *Documenting the Justice Gap in America* (Washington, D.C.: Legal Services Corporation, 2007).

Chapter 1: Lessons from the Good Samaritan

1. Richard Stearns, *The Hole in our Gospel* (Nashville: Thomas Nelson, 2009), 66.

2. Jim Wallis, *Faith Works: Lessons from the Life of an Activist Preacher* (New York: Random House, 2000), 71–72.

3. Stearns, *The Hole in our Gospel*.

4. *The Poverty and Justice Bible*, American Bible Society, New York 1995, Contemporary English Version.

5. This number represents those living below 125 percent of the federal poverty guideline, which is the standard used by many service providers, including legal service providers. Carmen DeNavas-Walt, Bernadette D. Proctor, and Jessica C. Smith, *U.S. Census Bureau, Current Population Reports*, 60-238; *Income, Poverty, and Health Insurance Coverage in the United States: 2010*, U.S. Government Printing Office, Washington, D.C. 2011, 19.

6. Lewis Powell Jr., Address to the American Bar Association Legal Services Program, ABA Annual Meeting, August 10, 1976.

7. *Documenting the Justice Gap in America* (Washington, D.C.: Legal Services Corporation, 2007).

8. Ibid.

Chapter 2: Lessons from the Injured

1. Kenneth W. Osbeck, *Amazing Grace, 366 Inspiring Hymn Stories for Daily Devotions* (Grand Rapids: Kregel Publications, 1990), 202.

2. Margueritte Bixler Garrett, *History and Message of Hymns* (Elgin, Ill.: The Elgin Press, 1924), 94–5.

3. David K. Shipler, *The Working Poor, Invisible in America* (New York: Alfred A. Knopf, 2004), 3–4.

4. 44.3 percent of children under the age of six living with a single mom were in poverty and 18.5 million of the poor were white compared with 12.4 million Hispanics, 9.9 million Blacks, and 1.7 million Asians. Carmen DeNavas-Walt, Bernadette D. Proctor, and Jessica C. Smith, *U.S. Census Bureau, Current Population Reports, 60-238; Income, Poverty, and Health Insurance Coverage in the United States: 2009,* U.S. Government Printing Office, Washington D.C. 2010, 16.

5. Children comprised 35.5 percent of people in poverty but only 24.5 percent of the total population. Ibid.

6. Based on the 2009 poverty rate of 14.3 percent.

7. Ibid., 14.

8. Ibid., 4.

9. The 2010 World Justice Project Rule of Law Index, www.worldjusticeproject.org/rule-of-law-index, released June 13, 2011, accessed June 19, 2011.

10. People 16 years and older who worked some or all of 2009 had a lower poverty rate than those who did not work at any time—6.9 percent compared with 22.7 percent. In 2009, the poverty rate among full-time, year-round workers was lower than the rate for those who worked part-time or part-year—2.7 percent compared with 13.5 percent. Those who did not work in 2009 represented 43.0 percent of people in poverty and 25.8 percent of all people. Carmen DeNavas-Walt, Bernadette D. Proctor, and Jessica C. Smith, 15, 17–18.

11. Households with those who had lower levels of education were more likely to remain in or move into a lower quintile than households that had higher levels of education. Ibid., 4.

12. Ronald J. Sider, *Just Generosity* (Grand Rapids,: Baker Books 2007), 43–50.

Chapter 3: Lessons from the Robbers

1. Mortgage Asset Research Institute, *Twelfth Periodic Mortgage Fraud Case Report*, April 2010.

2. *Paying More for the American Dream IV: The Decline of Prime Mortgage Lending in Communities of Color.* May 2010.

3. Heartland Alliance Mid-America Institute on Poverty, *2009 Report on Chicago Region Poverty*, 7.

4. Monsignor John Egan's campaign in Illinois to address such injustice resulted in legislation to end exorbitant interest on payday loans and installment loans, HB 537. A broad coalition of religious, community and legal groups advocated for the change, which took effect in March 2011. For loans with terms of six months or less, the law caps rates at $15.50 per

$100 borrowed every two weeks, ensures the loan does not extend beyond 180 days with no balloon payment, eliminates hidden fees, and limits repayment terms to no more than 25 percent of a borrower's gross monthly income. For loans with terms more than six months' interest is capped at 99 percent for loans less than $4,000 and 36 percent for loans over $4,000, limits repayment terms to no more than 22.5 percent of a borrower's gross monthly income, and prohibits balloon payments.

5. *Diverted Opportunity. Refund Anticipation Loans Drain Wealth from Low Wealth Tax Filers and Communities of Color,* Woodstock Institute, January 2010, 2.

6. Ibid., 1.

7. Centers for Disease Control and Prevention, *Adverse Health Conditions and Health Risk Behaviors Associated with Intimate Partner Violence—United States 2005.*

8. Centers for Disease Control and Prevention, *Behavioral Risk Factor Surveillance System Survey, 2005.*

9. Centers for Disease Control and Prevention, *Adverse Health Conditions and Health Risk Behaviors Associated with Intimate Partner Violence—United States 2005.*

10. National Research Panel to Review Risk and Prevalence of Elder Abuse and Neglect. *Elder Mistreatment: Abuse, Neglect and Exploitation in an Aging America* (Washington D.C.: National Academies Press, 2003).

11. Fact Sheet: *Elder Abuse Prevalence and Incidence,* National Center on Elder Abuse, Washington D.C., 2005.

12. *Child Maltreatment 2008,* U.S. Department of Health and Human Services, Administration for Children and Families, 25.

13. Ibid., 28.

14. This is a strong and continuing theme through Scripture. For just a few of the many verses, examine Exodus 22:21–22; Deuteronomy 24:14, 17, 25:13–15; Psalm 94, 10:1–2, 14–15, 17–18, 14:6, 35:10, 58:1–2, 72:4,12, 140:12; Proverbs 13:23, 22:16, 22–23; Ecclesiastes 4:1, 5:8; Isaiah 10:1–2, 58:3,6,9–10, 61:8; Jeremiah 20:12–13, 21:12, 22:3,13; Ezekiel 22:29–30, 45:9-10; Amos 2:7,4:1; Malachi 3:5; James 5:4.

15. *Trafficking in Persons Report,* 10th edition, Department of State, June 2010, 338–44.

16. Ibid., 341

Chapter 4: Lessons from the Priest

1. See Luke 1:8, 23.

2. Udo Middelmann, *Christianity versus Fatalistic Religions in the War Against Poverty* (Colorado Springs: Paternoster Publishing, 2007), 193.

3. Magna Carta, 1215, paragraph 40.

4. Reginald Heber Smith, *Justice and the Poor* (New York: The Merrymount Press, 1919), 9.

5. Jacob Riis, *How the Other Half Lives: Studies among the Tenements of New York*, (Belknap Press, Harvard University, 2010, originally published in 1890).

6. Reginald Heber Smith, 8.

7. The German Immigration Society in 1890 expanded to include service to all low-income clients and became the Legal Aid Society of New York. That organization still exists and is the largest legal aid organization in the country.

8. The Bureau of Justice merged with The Protective Agency for Women and Children in 1905 and became the Chicago Legal Aid Society. In 1919 the organization became part of United Charities and was renamed Legal Aid Bureau. In 1995 the United Charities changed its name to Metropolitan Family Services, which remains the largest social service provider in Chicago.

9. Alan W. Houseman, Linda E. Perle, *Securing Equal Justice for All: A Brief History of Civil Legal Assistance in the United States* (Washington, D.C.: Center for Law and Social Policy, revised January 2007), 11.

10. Smith, 151.

11. Houseman and Perle, 16.

12. The legal services corporation is primarily funded by the federal government and distributes these funds to 136 independent legal aid programs across the country with 900 offices. www.lsc.gov/about/factsheet_whatislsc.php, accessed July 7, 2010.

13. David Claerbaut, *The Reluctant Defender* (Carol Stream, Ill.: Tyndale House, 1978), 54–6. The projects of Cabrini Green, the neighborhood in which Chuck and Bill Leslie fought hard to win the hearts and souls of the residents, no longer exists. The city of Chicago revitalized the area with upscale condominiums. Cabrini Green Legal Aid continues to serve residents of Chicago from the near northwest side. See www.cgla.net.

14. John Robb identifies ten key leaders in his recent book: Chuck Hogren, frequently referred to as the father of Christian Legal Aid; Sam and Jill Casey, who led Christian Legal Society and worked with John Robb in promoting CLA across the country; Alan Sears, the president of Alliance Defense Fund for leading that fund and providing major financial support to CLS and its Christian Legal Aid work; Gerry Nordgren, a long-time Christian Legal Aid attorney with Austin Law Center in Chicago; Andy Toles, for his work in Seattle and nationally; Abigail "Abby" Kuzma, a national Christian Legal Aid leader and the past director of Neighborhood Christian Legal Clinic in Indianapolis. See www.nclegalclinic.org; Tom Rulon, who began one of the early programs at the Honolulu Rescue Mission and developed some of the important early tools; Anna Waldherr, for full-time volunteer work in Philadelphia; Gordon Beggs, a law professor for advocating rights of the poor; and Bruce Strom and Administer Justice, for communicating a needed holistic gospel justice approach to Christian

Legal Aid which no one has effectively done before. John D. Robb, *Defending the Poor with the Love of God* (self-published, 2010), 105–12.

15. John Robb estimated that by 2006, church agency sponsored Christian Legal Aid programs served only about one-third of the total number of clients being assisted in the CLS network. Robb, 76.

16. Ibid., 9.

17. Ibid., 66.

Chapter 5: Lessons from the Levite

1. Leviticus 21:11.

2. John 8:1–11.

3. See John 4:4–42.

4. See also Deuteronomy 16:14; 26:12–13.

5. Acts 4:36.

6. 1 Corinthians 10:24.

7. "He who gives to the poor will lack nothing, but he who closes his eyes to them receives many curses" (Proverbs 28:27). See also Proverbs 21:13: "If a man shuts his ears to the cry of the poor, he too will cry out and not be answered."

8. *Documenting the Justice Gap in America* (Washington, D.C.: Legal Services Corporation, 2007).

9. Peacemaker Ministries was founded in 1982 under the auspices of the Christian Legal Society, which helped establish many similar ministries. In 1987, many of these conciliation ministries joined to form the Association of Christian Conciliation Services (ACCS), which in 1993 merged into Peacemaker Ministries. Peacemaker Ministries continues to work closely with Christian Legal Society, national church ministries, and others in training God's people to reconcile and restore relationships by responding to conflict biblically. See www.peacemaker.net.

10. Ken Sande with Tom Raabe, *Peacemaking for Families, A Biblical Guide to Managing Conflict in Your Home* (Carol Stream, Illinois: Tyndale House Publishers, 2002), 12.

11. Romans 14:10–12.

Chapter 6: Lessons from the Samaritan

1. David Noel Freedman, *The Anchor Bible Dictionary* (New York: Doubleday, 1996), 5:941.

2. Ezra 4.

3. Nehemiah 6.

4. The 2009 Honesty and Ethics Poll ranked Congressmen as worst, followed by used car salesmen. Only 13 percent of people polled had a positive view of lawyers, with 40 percent having a very low view. *Gallup Honesty and*

Ethics Poll online at www.gallup.com/poll/124625/Honesty-Ethics-Poll-Finds-Congress-Image-Tarnished.aspx, accessed August 23, 2010.

5. Christian Buckley and Ryan Dobson, *Humanitarian Jesus: Social Justice and the Cross* (Chicago: Moody Publishers, 2010), 71.

6. Ibid., 145.

7. Max Lucado, interview on his book, *Outlive Your Life: You Were Made to Make a Difference*, www.christianbook.com/Christian/Books/cms_content?page=863618&event=PR, accessed August 20, 2010.

8. Randy Alcorn, *The Treasure Principle, Unlocking the Secret of Joyful Giving*, (Sisters, Ore.: Multnomah Books, 2001), 32.

9. Charles Dickens, *A Christmas Carol*.

Chapter 7: Lessons from the Jericho Road

1. Several passages reflect God's justice including Psalm 9:8, Psalm 33:5, Psalm 36:6; Isaiah 9:7, Isaiah 16:5, Isaiah 30:18.

2. Psalm 111:7; Isaiah 5:16, Isaiah 33:5, Isaiah 42:1–4, Isaiah 51:4–5; Zephaniah 3:5.

3. Psalm 45:6, Psalm 89:14, Acts 17:31; 1 Peter 4:5; Revelation 19:11.

4. Michael O. Emerson and Christian Smith, *Divided by Faith: Evangelical Religion and the Problem of Race in America* (New York: Oxford University. Press, 2000).

5. Edward Gilbreath, *Reconciliation Blues, A Black Evangelical's Inside View of White Christianity* (Downers Grove, Ill.: Intervarsity Press, 2006), 155.

6. Bruce Wilkinson, "The Way from Jerusalem to Jericho," *The Biblical Archaeologist,* Vol. 38, No. 1 (Mar. 1975), 10–24.

7. Eileen Ambrose, "Zombie Debt: Debt Can Come Back to Haunt You Years Later," *The Baltimore Sun,* May 6, 2007, 1C.

8. Internal Revenue Code, 26 USC 7701(b).

9. *Social Security Number and Individual Taxpayer Identification Number Mismatches and Misuse,* Hearing before the subcommittee on oversight and subcommittee on Social Security of the Committee on Ways and Means, U.S. House of Representatives, One Hundred Eighth Congress, second session, March 10, 2004, 2.

10. Eduardo Porter, "Immigrants pad books, balance social security," *New York Times,* April 10, 2005.

11. *Social Security Number and Individual Taxpayer Identification Number Mismatches and Misuse, 2.*

12. Matthew Soerens and Jenny Hwang, *Welcoming the Stranger: Justice, Compassion, and Truth in the Immigration Debate* (Downers Grove, Ill.: InterVarsity Press, 2009).

13. Daniel Carroll, *Christians at the Border: Immigration, the Church and the Bible* (Grand Rapids: Baker Academic, 2008).

14. The Development, Relief and Education for Alien Minors Act would permit the opportunity to earn conditional permanent residency if they complete two years in the military or two years at a four-year institution of higher learning. The bill was defeated in 2001 and after passing the House, failed in the Senate in December 2010. In 2012 President Obama issued an executive order commonly referred to as DACA—Deferred Action for Childhood Arrivals—which puts a halt to deportation of certain children of undocumented immigrants and, under certain guidelines, a path to work authorization. See www.uscis.gov/childhoodarrivals. But without congressional action, such an executive order could be removed, leaving these young people exposed to deportation.

Chapter 8: Lessons from the Inn

1. Paul David Tripp, *Instruments in the Redeemer's Hands* (Phillipsburg, N.J.: P&R Publishing, 2002), 116.

2. David Claerbaut, *The Reluctant Defender* (Wheaton, Ill.: Tyndale, 1978), 238.

3. Philip Yancey, *Church: Why Bother? My Personal Pilgrimage* (Grand Rapids: Zondervan, 1998), 31.

4. David Platt, *Radical* (Colorado Springs: Multnomah Books, 2010), 198.

5. Timothy Keller, *Generous Justice, How God's Grace Makes Us Just* (New York: Penguin Group, 2010), 142.

6. "Strained Suburbs: The Social Service Challenges of Rising Suburban Poverty," published by the Metropolitan Policy Program at the Brookings Institute, October 2010.

7. www.u-46.org/cdps/cditem.cfm?nid=14.

8. McKinney-Vento Homeless Assistance Act, 42 USC 11431.

9. Keller, *Generous Justice,* 135.

10. Tony Evans, *Oneness Embraced* (Chicago: Moody Publishers, 2011), 265.

11. Yancey, *Church: Why Bother?,* 30.

12. Platt, *Radical,* 170.

13. Ronald J. Sider, Philip N. Olson, and Heidi Rolland Unruh, *Churches That Make a Difference* (Grand Rapids: Baker Books, 2002), 314.

14. The Gospel Coalition, http://thegospelcoalition.org/about/foundation-documents/vision/.

15. Max Lucado, *Outlive Your Life* (Nashville: Thomas Nelson, 2010), 106.

Chapter 9: Lessons from the Lawyer

1. David J. Moraine, "Loyalty Divided: Duties to Clients and Duties to Others—the Civil Liability of Tax Attorneys Made Possible by Acceptance of a Duty to the System," *The Tax Lawyer,* Volume 63, No. 1, Fall 2009, American Bar Association, 169.

2. Melanie Acevedo, "Client Choices, Community Values: Why Faith-Based Legal Services Providers Are Good for Poverty Law," *Fordham Law Review*, Vol. 70 (2002), 1491.

3. Benjamin Cardozo, *Nature of the Judicial Process* quoted in *Lloyd's Introduction to Jurisprudence*, 5th ed. Lord Lloyd of Hampstead and M.D.A. Freeman (London: Stevens & Sons, 1985), 1179.

4. Christian Buckley and Ryan Dobson, *Humanitarian Jesus: Social Justice and the Cross* (Chicago: Moody Publishers, 2010), 161.

5. *Documenting the Justice Gap in America* (Washington, D.C.: Legal Services Corporation, 2007), 4.

6. Ibid.

7. Reginald Heber Smith, *Justice and the Poor* (New York: The Merrymount Press, 1919), 31.

8. Ibid, 241.

9. Based on statistics in Illinois, which are suggestive of other states. In 2009 there were 87,087 attorneys registered in Illinois, who reported performing 1,113,778 hours of legal service directly to those of limited means. Using a 40-hour work week for those attorneys, divided by the hours donated, reveals that on average each attorney spent 0.006 percent of time doing *pro bono* work for the indigent. *Attorney Registration and Disciplinary Commission of the Supreme Court of Illinois Annual Report 2009*, 12.

10. This is a national statistic reported by the American Bar Association. The ABA Standing Committee on Pro Bono and Public Service, *Supporting Justice: A Report on the Pro Bono Work of America's Lawyers*, August 2005, 17.

11. Canon 18 Professional Rules of Ethics, 2 Am. Law School Revelation, 230, 232.

12. J. George Sharwood: *An Essay on Professional Ethics* (Littleton, Colo.: F. B. Rotham, fifth edition, 1993 [1854]), 53.

13. Ronald J. Sider, Philip N. Olson, and Heidi Rolland Unruh, *Churches That Make a Difference* (Grand Rapids: Baker Books, 2002), 130.

14. Timothy Keller, *Generous Justice, How God's Grace Makes Us Just* (New York, NY: Penguin Group, 2010), 93–4.

Chapter 10: Lessons from Jesus

1. www.census.gov/hhes/www/poverty/indExodushtml.

2. Amber Van Schooneveld, *Hope Lives: A Journey of Restoration* (Loveland, Colo.: Group Publishing, 2008), 56.